LIVING LOVE:

FINDING TRUE JOY, FREEDOM AND PEACE

TRUE HENDERSON

Hawthorne Publishing
Carmel, Indiana

Hawthorne Publishing
15601 Oak Road
Carmel, Indiana 46033

ISBN: 0-9726273-2-4

CONTENTS

Part Four - The Power of Love To Heal

Part Five—Living Love Brings True Freedom

ACKNOWLEDGMENTS

I am deeply grateful to my family and friends who have stood by me over these last few years as I have "adventured" into a new and dynamic way of living life.

Thank you to my children, Craden, Shaun, Kerri and Debbie, and my in-law children, Jessica, Jessica, Max and Ben, for always believing in me and carrying me through those times when I lost my way and forgot to believe in myself. Thank you for keeping me on track and never giving up on me. You are each so amazing.

My heartfelt appreciation goes to daughter and son-in-law, Kerri and Max Martina, with whom I have lived and played during much of the writing process. Max has been my meticulous editor as well as my visionary mentor and guide. Kerri continues to work as my dedicated sales and accounting manager.

Special thanks to my other daughter, Debbie, for her professional expertise and flair in designing both the cover of *Living Love* and my website.

I am in awe of the enduring love and caring of the many other friends, mentors and guides who have stood by me along the way—most especially (and in somewhat chronological order) Emmanuel Carper, Evelyn Norton, Kit and Ruth Robison, Mary Hunt, Jessica Fleming, Nan Brine, Susanne Sharpe, Tom Russell, Jim and June Spencer. You are my heroes.

Thank you to those special friends who read various editions of the manuscript and provided such constructive and inspired criticism and support—particularly those not already mentioned, Margaret Powell, Kim Smith, and Emma O'Loughlin.

And to all the other people who have helped seed ideas and encouraged me in new directions, my deepest appreciation. You have all been catalysts for making *Living Love* a reality.

INTRODUCTION

Imagine for a moment that we all live and breathe, not in an atmosphere of life-sustaining air, but in an atmosphere of life-sustaining Love, an atmosphere of unchanging harmony. Imagine this atmosphere of harmony or Love is not just around this planet and universe, but is everywhere, infinite—without beginning or end. Imagine, too, that this atmosphere of infinite harmony is a principle or law of Love that holds each one of us in perfect health and peace. We can never be outside this atmosphere of Love, and never beyond this state of complete synergy because it is our natural, normal state of being.

This is the key (and the point of departure from many of the world's belief systems): ultimate reality is spiritual, not physical. We are not physical bodies but divine spiritual beings dwelling in the atmosphere of harmony, Love—although at present we may be asleep to this knowing.

"What sort of idealism is this?" you ask. "Look at what is all around us—disturbance, violence, discord, unhappiness, chance, accident, sickness, limitation—everything that is completely opposed to such a picture of harmony." But suppose that this picture of limitation is something humanity is conditioned to believe, a sort of dream-state resulting from losing sight of our higher selfhood, a higher reality. This dream has persisted for so long that we have no recollection of anything different. We are caught in the mesmerism of mass consciousness that believes this is the way life is and that we have no real control over the events of our lives, our happiness, health or success. This conditioning is so complete that we passively accept the inevitability of discord and disturbance in this thing we call our life.

What if living with discord and limitation is not inevitable? What if, right now, we have a choice as to how we want our lives to be? Is it possible this is true? Yes. I know, as do many others, that it is possible to choose how we want our lives to be—*if* we are willing to wake up to, and *live,* the truth of who we really are: spiritual beings living in an atmosphere, a spiritual universe even, of harmony and love.

The more we wake up to remember our true spiritual identity

and consciously live the love that is inherent in us as divine spiritual beings, the more the events of our human lives mirror our increasing awareness of harmony and love. We discover how to live this spiritual awareness with increasing fulfillment and wonder. We discover that our radiant, unique identities include not only who we are but also what we came here to do, our true purpose. Then at last we find what it is that makes our hearts sing and our eyes light up, and life becomes a magnificent dance full of power and promise.

Creating an extraordinary life of harmony and fulfillment, abundant in good health, joy, freedom and peace, cannot be achieved simply by intellectualizing spiritual truths. Creating an extraordinary life requires getting to *feeling* a sense of love that cannot even be expressed in words or logical thinking. From this feeling flows a necessity for *living love* in our lives, gifting to others as well as to ourselves kindness, acceptance, patience, and the many other qualities of unconditional love.

When we live in this way, when we are *living love,* we surely find the joy of discovering our identity and source, we find freedom from disease, limitation and emotional wounds that bind us, and we find the peace of an active discovery that nourishes our soul. We can choose a whole new world of our own creating. It really is up to *us!*

This book, *Living Love,* is intended to give spiritual seekers new insights into how to practice the day-to-day living of the healing truths that so many profoundly inspirational books are now talking about. Intended also for those of you who are searching for a greater sense of identity and purpose, my hope is that this book will help give you courage in stepping out from what spiritual intuitive and author, Carolyn Myss calls "the tribe"—stepping out from the socially prescribed ways of doing life—as you come fully into your unique identity and purpose.

Living Love shares some of my answers to the big questions of life such as "what is Truth," "who am I" and "what am I here to do," as well as practical guidance on living with these answers. *Living Love* also explains how each one of us can discard—heal—anything in our lives that no longer serves us. Based on my own intimate and personal experience, and the experiences of people I have worked with, it is not intended to be a deep metaphysical study text, or to be extravagant in its promises, but to encourage you to listen to your own heart and follow your own inner guidance.

There is no set blueprint for our journey to truth. Because we each have a unique path to follow that has few signposts along the way, it makes no sense to spend our lives searching for someone who can tell us exactly how and where to go. We must find our own path. We must trust what our hearts and souls tell us via our *intuitions, feelings and emotions*. Such trust may make little sense to our intellectual and logical minds, but remember: *the heart knows what the mind refuses to believe.*

PART ONE

INSIGHTS

FROM MY OWN SPIRITUAL JOURNEY

CHAPTER 1

DISCOVERING MY TRUE IDENTITY

AND PURPOSE

Life is either a daring adventure or nothing at all.
Helen Keller

F INDING JOY AND FREEDOM HAS BEEN A LIFELONG PASSION OF mine. Even when I was very young I loved to do things that were creative and exciting. All my summers were spent at gorgeous New Zealand beaches swimming, exploring rock pools, climbing cliffs, wandering through forests, buildings forts and huts, camping, and in my early teen years, galloping my horse along the beach and swimming on her in the waves. They were precious years of freedom.

I will always be grateful that my parents were so trusting—well, usually. There was the time when my brother and I, at the ripe age of nine, built a raft out of driftwood that had been washed up on the ocean beach at which we were vacationing. After tying everything together with some waterlogged rope we found, we sailed off to sea. It was a short adventure as the waves became rather mountainous once we left the sheltered bay. We were forced to come ashore on a rocky platform below some ominous cliffs. Undeterred, we built a little fire and cooked crabs before negotiating the sheer ascent. The only scary part, as I remember, was that, as we bushwhacked our way through the dense forest at the top of the cliffs, my brother insisted a wild boar was going to eat me. When we reached home at nightfall we were, needless to say, in a lot of trouble as a search party had been called in to find us.

I grew up convinced that life is an adventure and people are supposed to be happy. Why? Because happiness, joy and freedom are our natural states of being. I can still remember as a child stubbornly trying to persuade my mother of this, but she used to mistake this notion as a rather regrettable selfishness in me, assuming that by happiness I meant a desire to acquire "things" that would make me happy. I knew this was not what I meant at all but I didn't have the language or reasoning skills to correct her misapprehension. With the wisdom of years I now know what I intuitively knew then—that deep inner joy is something we are all able and naturally inclined to express. If we can't feel this joy, and the freedom and peace that come from it, then we're missing some understanding essential to our well being. This inner peace and fulfillment, joy and freedom, I have discovered, comes from living the fullness of who we truly are, doing what we love to do. And we're all different—some peaceful and still, some noisy and active, many somewhere in between.

Each one of us has a unique identity and purpose in the entirety of all Creation. In truth, while this unique identity is spiritual, to our present human perception of things this identity takes form as a physical body that holds the essence of who we are and what we are here to do. Discovering our unique identity and purpose is essential to an enriching and fulfilling life.

It seems as if the spiritual teachings of all indigenous cultures, at least those of which I am aware, stress the importance of finding the true purpose for which we came into this life, knowing that no one can give of their full potential until this purpose is uncovered. For many Native Americans, the vision quest, originally part of the initiation of young warriors, was one such means of finding this purpose and vision. In a favorite book of mine, *Song of the Circle*, author Barry Brailsford, refers to how early indigenous peoples, such as those in New Zealand, were led to uncover their unique purpose. Of course it refers to all of us.

"Find your excitement. I say again, find your excitement and follow it. Honour only that which gives you joy and brings energy and purpose to your life. Then you walk the truth of who you are. Then you walk the magic and the dream."

When we know what we are passionate about doing in this life, when we have a clear sense of our purpose, we feel comfortable in our skin—our unique identity is clear to us. Likewise, when we uncover a satisfying answer to the question, "who am I"—when we feel we know what constitutes our unique identity—we can quickly discover our purpose. Our mission and direction then become clear. Thus, purpose and identity are fully intertwined and understanding one without the other becomes impossible.

While our purpose is something that is inherent in how we think and act, it is surprising how many of us have little or no idea what this purpose is. I know from my own life journey that we may spend much of our lives wandering from one job to another searching for something that seems to fit who we are. Once discovered however, we realize our purpose is actually something that has resonated with us most of our lives; it is often something so natural to us that it either went unnoticed or we really didn't think we could make a career of it. And yet when I think about the happiest, most fulfilled and successful people I know, without exception all of them are doing what they truly love to do—their work seems to them like play. Purpose and identity are in sync.

As Abraham Maslow, the famous psychologist, once said, "A musician must make his music, an artist must paint, a poet must write, if he is to ultimately be at peace with himself." Finding our peace certainly includes finding our purpose and true identity.

This intensive search for identity and meaning is a relatively recent phenomenon in our society. It is a search that looks to many, particularly to the older generations, like a downhill slide into self-indulgence and hedonism. Usually out of necessity, these people have been largely preoccupied with the practicalities of providing food on the table and a roof overhead, more often than not supported in their endeavors by a generally held belief that selflessness is the pathway to heaven. And yet, as I discuss throughout these pages, the search for an authentic sense of identity, while sometimes hedonistic, is usually anything but. More and more people are waking up to the realization that it is impossible to understand identity and purpose from a purely materialistic standpoint. Identity and purpose in this human experience can only be truly understood as we gain a growing understanding of our spiritual identity and higher purpose. Consequently, a deeply earnest spiritual search for greater meaning is preoccupying the minds of an increasing number of people every day.

While people have always embarked on spiritual journeys, the growing numbers of books and workshops about this search for identity and meaning indicate a significant trend. According to the results of a survey conducted over a number of years and published in 2000 in *The Cultural Creatives: how 50 million Americans are changing the world*, authors Dr. Paul Ray and Dr. Sherry Anderson show that since the 1960s 50 million Americans, 26% of the population, have made a complete shift in their values and way of life. Close to 50% of this number (25 million Americans) are more educated, leading edge thinkers who have strong values of personal growth and spirituality. A similar survey in 1997 indicated comparable percentages across Europe.

Ray and Anderson also noted that the majority of these "cultural creatives" felt quite alone on their journey, not realizing how many other people were seeking more authentic lives. I like to quote these statistics when individuals tell me either that there is no hope for our society or that we are on a slippery slide to extinction.

If a quarter of the U.S. population is seriously trying, from an individual, grassroots starting point, to create less materialistic, more harmonious lifestyles, then the effect of this critical mass has tremendous potential to radically change society, particularly as individuals realize they are not alone and can work together.

Protesting the idea that life is meant to be a struggle and a burden, many spiritual seekers are finding that they actually can learn to discard— heal—whatever is discordant in their lives. They find they can live extraordinarily fulfilling lives of joy, freedom and peace when they discover who they really are and what they are here to do. And they also find that from their own search for meaning comes a profound need to help others do the same. These peace-promoting results are global.

Of course developing greater self-awareness is not a new idea. In ancient Greece, temples were inscribed with the well-known advice, "know thyself." With the ensuing evolving consciousness, this self-knowing is now taking a more spiritual direction.

Looking back on my life I can see that my purpose, and therefore my sense of identity has clearly unfolded right from my earliest childhood. I see now my purpose has always been what I love to do most—to discover more and more about living love, about finding true joy, freedom and peace. Although I have been living this purpose since I was little, it has only been in recent years that I have become fully conscious of it. My professional career now embraces learning and teaching how to heal whatever does not belong in an atmosphere of love—for instance, unhappiness, sickness, financial difficulties, relationship challenges and career setbacks.

This process of becoming conscious of my life purpose has also enabled me to understand more about who I am. Or it might be that setting out to discover more about my true identity has enabled me to become conscious of my life purpose. These processes really are two sides of the same coin.

I have always loved to be around other people. Even when I was very small, I could often feel a wellspring of joy bubbling up from inside me and flowing out to the people around me. This upwelling feels like an uncontrollable urge to express a joy that reaches out and releases the joy in others. I want so much for people to feel that joy, and even when I am with someone who is grieving or despondent, I usually find something to think or say that will lift them up and clear some of the heaviness.

Now that I am able to understand inner feelings that, in earlier years, were quite unconscious, I see how, even when I was very little, I understood a whole lot about my spiritual selfhood. Because both my mother and grandparents followed the teachings of Christian Science, I grew up learning that God has created us in his image and likeness as spiritual beings.

[Note: I use the word "God" here because that is the term for the one infinite and eternal principle of creation that I grew up with. I understand my sense of God differs greatly from that used by many religions. Often I use other terms like "the power of infinite Love," depending on the sense of this God power I have at the time. You will also notice I capitalize words like Love when I'm referring to God. I also refer to God sometimes as he, sometimes as she simply because we don't have a word that means both of these. "It" is too impersonal.]

I grew up being taught that God is infinite Love, never creating or seeing anything that is not loving and beautiful. I also learned that he does not create or see anything in this human existence—a human existence which is simply the outcome of our expectations and beliefs. I learned that anything unlike good is not part of God's creation and therefore not a part of spiritual reality. Also, because God is good and is All, a secondary power of evil or discord cannot exist, except in this dream-state that we call our human life.

I will expand on these ideas throughout the book, but for now the above brief outline of some of the spiritual truths I was taught explains why I grew up with such an innate and unshakeable belief that love and harmony are my, and everyone else's, natural state of being. When my friends seemed anxious and afraid of illness, accident, and all sorts of other problems, I was quite convinced that, although I occasionally had minor childhood illnesses, there was nothing that could ever happen to me that could seriously harm me. As a little child, I remember often thinking, "if only people could see who they really are there would be no fear, anger and hurt, no war, no violence." I suppose I wanted to help them remember what in truth, as spiritual beings, they had always known.

Even when I was quite young, I had a solid conviction that love —and therefore joy, freedom and peace—is infinitely abundant, eternal, without limits, and therefore available to all. Nor are there limited resources for an overpopulated planet. When we learn that good is infinitely abundant, when we change our perception of limitation to one of infinite supply, this heightened awareness of harmony causes us to manifest exactly what we need to sustain and maintain all creation in perfect balance. We are dealing with thoughts not things. This is what it means to *live love*—to live each day in spontaneous gratitude for the understanding of spiritual abundance and freedom rather than unwittingly accepting a fearful delusion of material limitation.

As I matured, I felt a growing compulsion to understand more and more about authentic love—not the temporary and elusive ideas of love the media in particular associates with finding happiness—the right friends, the right partner, the right job, the right income, house, car, possessions—although that too had preoccupied me for awhile. No, my growing compulsion was to understand the nature of the love that filled me with a sense of deep joy and purpose, rippling out and filling everyone it touched with a new light, awakening them to remember their true selfhood as pure and unique expressions of infinite Love.

It gradually dawned on me that love is a *feeling*, an emotion that is so vast that there is no way it can be comprehended in words or by intellectual argument. Only through *feeling* this love can we come close to comprehending its magnitude and its power to heal and harmonize.

I realized how this love is the divine energy of God radiating out from a consciousness of joy and peace, and it could touch even the most stubborn fear and anger in the world, thus creating peace. I discovered this first by sending love "energy" to people around me. I saw people begin to smile and lighten up even when I wasn't talking to them.

Sitting in an airport lounge a few years ago with a close friend who also understands these ideas, I suggested that we occupy ourselves while waiting for a delayed flight by seeing if we could cheer up some of the stressed, sad looking people who were passing by. We didn't plan to interact in any conscious way with them, but just to focus on radiating our shared energies of love and seeing everyone around us as divine, spiritual expressions of this Love. We found ourselves quietly laughing together as the familiar sense of joy bubbled up and out. Almost immediately we noticed people slowing to look at us, surprised perhaps by the sense of warmth and joy we were sharing. Some people smiled, others just seemed to grow taller as their burdens lightened. And there were those who turned away and hurried on, determined not to be moved from their resolve to stay in the illusion of unhappiness. I've found myself radiating love in this way many times since with the same results. Love has a way of creeping in unannounced.

Radiating love, allowing the divine energy of God to pour through us in this way, also has the power to heal physical problems instantly. One night recently I went to bed suddenly feeling very sick. I had a splitting headache, upset stomach, and couldn't breathe easily. Nor could I find any clarity of thought to pray, to see through this illusion of discord. I slept fitfully until early morning, and then, feeling no better, called a friend. I had hardly finished telling him what was wrong, when I felt an almost overpowering rush of love hit me as he reminded me how much I was loved, how I was literally at one with the power of divine Love, and how nothing could take away my joy and dominion. I felt as if I was being wrapped in a blanket of love as I snuggled back into bed and fell into a deep sleep. When I woke several hours later I was completely well.

Perhaps the most compelling example of radiating love happened to me the day after the Twin Towers attack in New York, September 11, 2001. A group of us came together to pray silently for peace and healing in the world. We sat around a low table of lighted candles listening to a friend quietly playing the harp. In the stillness, the music was so captivating as I prayed to see each person on this planet as the pure expression of Love. I prayed to see that there are no outcasts in God's creation of harmony, no misfits. I saw that when we forget our true selfhood as Love's expression, fear appears with all its associated manifestations of anger and hatred and revenge. I saw also that anger and hatred are never the natural status for anyone. I affirmed that, as each of us awakens to remember who we truly are, all hurt and fear disappear.

This is healing, as I know it: to remember our true spiritual selfhood as the very essence of Love—to simply remember what is already true—our present perfection.

As I prayed in this way, listening to the music, I imagined a white curling mist of the sound waves from the music and the thought waves of love moving around the room and then upwards and out of the ceiling. I felt as though this energy of love and joy was circling the whole earth, and settling onto everyone. It seemed first to settle on all the people affected by the horrors of the day before, instilling a sweet sense of peace and calm. It settled on the decision-makers in

Washington D.C., some of whom were trying, amidst all the confusion, condemnation and judgment, to make wise and compassionate choices. Then moving over the deserts of the Middle East, it seemed to come to rest over the so-called terrorists and religious fanatics. They looked up in surprise at the sound of the music, and as their hearts opened to the exquisite sound, the power of Love poured in, replacing fear and fury with quiet peace and joy.

I was so entranced by this feeling of love and by the looks of amazement on the faces of the people in my vision, that I couldn't help laughing in delight at the way Love had planted the seeds of hope and healing into even the most anguished hearts.

Since then, I've felt a heightened sense of healing going on throughout the world. There are so many people now involved in changing the face of fear and hurt to one of joy, freedom and peace. Such healing is possible when we know we're just waking up to what as always been true.

CHAPTER 2

HOW I LEARNED TO HEAL

Feeling is the language of the soul.
Neil Donald Walsch

GROWING UP IN A FAMILY THAT PRACTICED THE TEACHINGS OF Christian Science, I learned early on to rely wholly on prayer for all health care and other challenges. I learned early—and accepted for myself—that, in reality, there is just Love—the one Father-Mother God—and that there is no actual opposing evil entity or power of discord outside of my own consciousness able to disrupt my natural state of harmony. I came to see that, like all of us, I am the perfect spiritual evidence of all that Love is —joy, vitality, peacefulness, harmony and beauty. Even just a tiny glimpse of this truth was enough to restore this state of perfect harmony in my life and consistently and effectively heal everything I didn't want as part of my life, everything that seemed discordant.

I grew up accepting that matter (and all its associated limiting beliefs including genetics and heredity) is not the solid, tangible substance that most people believe it is. Many times I saw a sick body changed to a healthy one with no recovery time. I saw broken bones mended sometimes instantly. In other words, I saw that *matter can change form with a change of thought*—something, of course, that quantum physics is now proving. I saw how accidents, chance and environment, have no control over someone who chooses not to give them power. I saw that discord has no power other than the power we give it.

When I became ill with measles a few days before I was to go on a middle school trip I remember being certain I would be well enough to get a medical clearance in time to go. I did. When I was about sixteen I fell off my horse during a show jumping event and damaged my arm severely. I was determined I would be fine to ride two weeks later at the next event. I was. These outcomes weren't miracles to me: just natural and normal everyday occurrences.

I learned that the whole human experience is a dream state or thought projection. I have complete control over this illusion once I am aware of the limitation of the illusion. I can live contrary to those limitations as *I choose to live love*, to live in consonance with all Love's creation. I saw that to live a harmonious life requires emptying consciousness of inharmony—particularly letting go of any need to feel anger and fear. Choosing to live in a consciousness or atmosphere of love matters. Yes, it takes patience, but the results are incredible even when I only remember to live in this love consciousness occasionally.

I gradually saw this was true for everyone, not only for me. My friends would ask me why I often seemed so peaceful and somehow in control of my life, and I began to share with them what I was learning.

What I knew deep down inside was that, as it says in the first chapter of Genesis in the Bible, God had given me dominion over the whole earth. I saw clearly that this did not mean I had the right to plunder, conquer, destroy, annihilate or dishonor all the varied expressions of life on the planet. I saw clearly my desire to nurture, protect and honor all creation was part of my willingness to live love and to see through the eyes of love.

What I also knew deep down inside was that God had given me dominion over everything in this human experience. I knew that the account of man's downfall in the second chapter of the Bible is simply an allegory to describe what happens when we fall asleep and forget our spiritual perfection as God's pure and innocent children. I inherently knew that there was nothing that could ever happen to me that could take my innate joy and freedom from me.

The following experience helped me to really confirm this knowledge for myself.

When my two oldest children were babies I developed severe back pain that made carrying them—or doing anything for that matter—incredibly difficult. I suppose I could have taken the attitude that God had given me this burden to carry to remind me to slow down and be more humble. However, because I believe that God is a power rather than a benign (or to some people, a less than benign) type of father figure somewhere up above, I couldn't accept the notion that he sends sickness to teach us lessons or to punish us. On the other hand, I do believe that we draw discord into our experience to the extent it fills our consciousness. "We are our own thoughts" is a statement often heard today.

At the time I had this back problem I remember I had been suffering from a sense of burden about trying to cope with two little babies and be the perfect mother, the perfect wife, the perfect community and church person . . . and everything else perfect! I had a false sense of responsibility for keeping the whole world going.

Because I wasn't used to putting up with such physical suffering in my life, I set about healing this problem with the help of a spiritual healer, a Christian Science practitioner. She quickly noticed the sense of burden I had about my life. She also pointed out that, despite this picture or dream of discord, the truth about me was my ongoing spiritual perfection, completely untouched by the script of a human life.

As I realized what a bunch of limited and discordant thoughts I had accumulated, I was able to laugh at the whole situation. The mesmeric dream picture lost its hold in my thought. I realized I could choose to change the picture to one of harmony and joy. By the next morning I was completely free of any pain and have never had a problem with my back since. Neither have I fallen into the trap of believing I am responsible for holding up the whole world!

My own experiences led me to accept that healing is a normal every day occurrence, not something that is controlled by God's will. Healing is as natural as breathing and once we understand the power of Love and put this power into practice in our everyday life, healings will no longer seem like miracles nor things attempted as a last resort when all other remedies have failed.

Yes, I was starting to live what I was learning. I saw from experience that consistent healing did not happen through blind faith. And this is what I started to share with others when I was asked where my deep joy and stillness came from.

Despite this, learning how to heal did not come easily to me. I accepted other people could heal but for some reason I could not. I had a lot of mental or intellectual baggage in the way that prevented me from recognizing the simplicity of living love. I had plenty of ego control issues—thinking I was responsible for everyone and everything around me. I thought I always had to learn more, do more, become more, be more perfect and successful. Then I would be able to heal. I hadn't yet figured out that *being* who God has created me to be means living *effortlessly* how I feel most at ease and in my joy; to be as much as possible in the place where my heart sings and my eyes shine. I hadn't yet figured out that with such a love consciousness, naturally I would be able to heal and harmonize anything in my life that was not in accord with this love.

Although I had learned many of the principles of healing in my growing up years in a home where Christian Science healing was practiced, I found it really difficult to get from theory to practice, from a head place to a *feeling* place. I felt I *knew* "the truth" (whatever that means) and I could explain it quite easily but my intellectual logical mind didn't seem to be sufficient to produce consistent healing results. There seemed to be something missing but I did not know what. Obviously I did not know enough, I thought, so I would constantly study to know more.

I had grown up seeing and hearing of some amazing healings that had come about as a result of understanding the truths I had been taught and had read about, particularly in Mary Baker Eddy's book, *Science and Health*, which explains the concepts of Christian Science. I wondered why some people could heal, apparently quite easily, and others like me knew the same truths but didn't get the results. Yes, I was obviously missing something.

I would often think about the foundational truths that, when acknowledged and understood, seemed to allow healing to occur—

truths such as the Allness of God, good, and the illusory nature of matter and discord of any sort. I could readily accept the concept of God as the one power of infinite harmony or Love and the concept that all of Love's creation, including each one of us, is the evidence or manifestation of everything that God is. I could accept that my true selfhood is in perfect balance and harmony. I could accept that the dream state of this human experience is just that, a dream state or dreamscape from which I needed to awaken in order to see not only who I truly was but also who I have always been. I could see how remembering these truths brings healing. In fact, it is the healing itself.

I could accept that this one power of Love and harmony is also eternal, ageless Life. It is Principle, it is Truth itself, it is the one infinite Soul, Spirit, and Mind that is All that Is. I could understand how Eddy had chosen to use seven synonyms for the word God: Life, Truth, Love, Principle, Soul, Spirit, Mind. I saw many ways to describe and identify—to try to come to grips with—what God is. I was pretty good at reasoning all this through.

And then there was the concept of God as Father-Mother used to indicate not only her gentle caring and nurturing protection of each and every one of her children, each one of us, but also his strong and principled guidance of our lives. I had learned that as spiritual ideas we are one with Love. So how then could we think of God as caring for us and guiding us in this human dream existence of which she was not even aware?

And this, it started to dawn on me, was what I was missing. I could intellectualize all of the above ideas about God and his/her perfect spiritual expression, Man (in the generic sense of the word). I could understand Jesus' statement, "ye shall know the truth and the truth shall make you free", but perhaps I did not fully understand how this somewhat impersonal "knowing", this *power* of infinite harmony, could also be referred to as our Father-Mother. I mean, if God is a power or principle, how is he/she also this loving presence that cares for and nurtures us?

I started to realize that intellectualizing and rationalizing everything was not enough. While I could see that blind faith wasn't the answer either, there was something also to do with *feeling* and even *trusting* in something that I could not fully comprehend just in my mind. And as I would soon discover, it was all to do with *living love*, with *feeling* the nurturing, gentle presence of unconditional love, which is God. This understanding, I realized, was not from the head at all. It was from the heart and soul.

My first really tangible healing taught me a lot about the importance of feeling this love. My entire life had included almost total reliance on prayer for health care needs. Virtually the only time I'd been to a doctor was to have my children—ah yes, and twice when my fourth child was a baby and I'd decided the sky was falling down on me and I couldn't find my bearings. But otherwise I had always trusted in the power of prayer to fix anything discordant in my own life and the lives of my children. It wasn't that I couldn't go to a doctor (as many people believe the teachings of Christian Science dictate). I could have chosen to use medical help, but I just felt that relying on the power of prayer to heal would result in quicker, more consistent and effective results.

Despite this reliance on prayer for healing, I wasn't confident in my own ability to heal so I would always call a Christian Science practitioner/healer, usually my mother, for help.

Late one night when my youngest daughter was about twelve or thirteen, she came down from her bedroom to see me, very distressed and having difficulty breathing. She was frightened and so was I, particularly when neither my mother nor another practitioner answered the phone. I quickly realized this time I had no choice but to prove what I really did know: that each one of us has direct access to the healing truths of Love. Once we know these truths or even just glimpse them, we can forego any intermediaries. I suggested to Debbie that she cuddle back in her bed while I prayed.

As I sat there in the night stillness I thought, "Dear Father Mother, what do I need to know to really see this child of yours as you see her, spiritual and perfect now and forever?" I decided not to try and reason through some intellectual truths, but just to keep very still and listen until I could hear an answer from my higher consciousness, from God. Very soon the thought came clearly to me that I simply needed to see her entirely surrounded, encompassed, immersed in Love. I needed to *feel* this love gently enfolding her, enfolding me, enfolding this home, this planet. I needed to *feel* that this love is her love, my love, our very *being*. In this love I could see both of us as vibrant, living, spiritual beings, free and full of joy and delight, completely untouched by the illusions of this mortal, temporal dream state. I thought about all the qualities that Debbie expresses—joy, wisdom, creativity, sensitivity, energy, laughter, deep spirituality—and I saw that all these things are who she really is. They are part of her true identity. How could the lie of discord even touch this perfect, free spiritual being? This lie had no power over her; it had no substance to it. Awakening to remember these truths, I felt so inspired, so uplifted. I felt like laughing in the joy of this revelation.

At that moment Debbie came into the room half asleep to tell me she was all better, thank you very much, and that I should go to bed. I was overjoyed not just because she was well but also because I had been able to help her myself, and it had not been so difficult after all. At once I saw clearly it was all about love, *feeling Love's presence* — or, as Lyn Grabhorn says in her delightful book *Excuse Me, Your Life is Waiting*, feeeeeling.

From then on my trust in Love's gentle care grew quickly, and I learned that living love is the prerequisite to healing. There is nothing gained from talking about love if you don't live that feeling. The discord we experience is in direct proportion to the discord in our thinking. Likewise, the harmony we experience is in direct proportion to the harmony in our thought. Are we seeing through the eyes of love? Are we feeling the oneness of all creation? Do we believe in a power apart from God? Are we living fear, the fear that someone or something might destroy our happiness, that someone or something might hurt us, that we are at the mercy of something outside ourselves, even a devil?

Whatever is not love is fear and fear can manifest as anger, hatred and numerous other forms of fear-based thinking. If, however, we accept that there is just the one power of Love, of infinite harmony, then we see that fear-based thinking is simply part of the human dream existence—that there is just love.

And yet it seems reasonable to assume that there is something besides good, besides love. Look at all the chaos, hate, fear, starvation, disease and environmental destruction on the planet. How is it possible to say such devastation does not exist? Of course it exists! The more fundamental question is where does it exist. Is it possible this devastation exists merely in the mass consciousness of a world that has fallen asleep to its true identity? Is it possible that when even one person awakens to see what is really going on they free themselves from the dream and at the same time help awaken and heal others? While there have been many mystics and prophets throughout history who have awakened from this dream of inharmony, only now are we reaching a critical mass where sufficient numbers of people are glimpsing these truths for the effect to be planetary.

There are so many different ways of seeing and articulating the truth and the power of Love and we are each drawn to what best squares with our inner knowing. Some of us choose one particular pathway or teaching. Others draw on a wonderfully eclectic mix.

Growing up focusing almost exclusively on the teachings of Christian Science, it is only in recent years that I have begun to read more widely. I quickly discovered common threads in many different spiritual teachings and have come to appreciate the universal nature of truth. While the explanation of Christian Science found in *Science and Health* still provides a solid foundation for my spiritual understanding of truth and love, particularly in my healing work, I feel so blessed to have discovered such an exciting diversity of ways to express this truth.

One book that talks about some of the key points that I grew up learning in the teachings of Christian Science is *A Course in Miracles*. Published a century after *Science and Health*, while naturally using different terminology, it also makes the distinction between the real and the unreal— that truth, the law of love or God, is all that is real, while the world of perception, the world of time, of change, the world of birth and death, is illusion.

What perception sees and hears appears to be real because it permits into awareness only what conforms to the wishes of the perceiver

. . . . caught in the world of perception you are caught in a dream.

At the end of the day, whether we follow one teaching or many, it doesn't matter. What matters is that we all awaken to remember who we truly are as spiritual expressions of divine Love and, in so doing, help awaken all of humanity.

In recent years, I have come consciously and fully into my purpose, into a clear sense of my identity. As I explain in the next chapter, healing and teaching have become an integral part of what I loosely call my life guidance profession. I teach how unconditional love heals. I teach that this love is God, encompassing All, being All. I teach that when we see through the eyes of Love, when we possess the inner knowing that there is just love, and when we can feel this love, anything that is not love and loving disappears into nothingness.

This is healing—feeling all love and nothing else—revealing present perfection, the Oneness that is already present. To heal is to *feel* this oneness of ever-present Love, of which each one of us is the spiritual and perfect expression. Understanding the deeper implications of our unity enables us to begin *Living Love* and *finding true joy, freedom and peace*. When we live love, not only can we heal anything that is disruptive in our lives, including physical illnesses, but we also find the true joy that comes from knowing unconditional love. We find the freedom to be who we truly are, do what we are here to do, and find the peace that comes when we understand we are all One. This Oneness of perfect being is ours already and always has been. We each find living love just as soon as we are ready to.

We all have a unique identity that includes the vital part we play in this life—our purpose. Although not consciously aware of it most of my life, I have now come to realize that my purpose is to reveal love in whatever way and through whatever channels it may appear, regardless of form or philosophy and it has led me to write this book in order to share with others my passion and my purpose.

CHAPTER 3

ESTABLISHING MY HEALING AND TEACHING PRACTICE

Nothing real can be threatened.
Nothing unreal exists.
Herein lies the peace of God.

A Course in Miracles

MY COMMITMENT TO UNDERSTANDING MORE ABOUT LOVE BE-
gan as early as I can remember in my life. I continued to grow in my understanding and practice of the healing power of this Love through the years of motherhood, community life and career. I learned that to heal effectively and consistently required maintaining a consciousness filled with love and harmony, something I could manage to do a reasonable amount of the time, at least when I wasn't getting unnerved and hassled by raising four children and earning enough income to help pay for their education. I sometimes felt I was juggling so many balls at once that even thinking about questions of identity and purpose seemed pointless.

And yet we don't ever lose the sense of identity and purpose that is natural and obvious to us in our very early years, even though we may not be able to articulate it. This sense of identity and purpose just gets increasingly obscured over the years by layers of external pressures and expectations.

By the time the youngest of the children was off to college, I felt as if I could again start to think for myself. I realized it was time to unearth some of the half-forgotten questions surrounding who I was and what I was here to do. These questions had never been satisfactorily answered in my teens and twenties. I had married when I was just twenty and still in college, and had started a family at twenty-three. I was glad that I had happily committed myself to all those years of at-home mothering when the children were preschoolers. Even when they went off to school I had always chosen work that allowed for flexible hours. We'd had a lot of fun as a family, but that chapter of my life was over.

Who was I? What did I want for myself? Honestly, I had no idea. Although I was doing well with my professional career, I sensed that, even though my life was comfortable and fairly predictable, I could not continue down the same path. I began experiencing an increasing sense of discomfort and displacement.

Lives have an unnerving habit of suddenly changing direction, especially, it seems, when things are going smoothly. Sometimes this change of direction happens as a result of an epiphany or a striking change of perspective on life that precipitates a need to re-design our lives to match. And sometimes it happens the other way around. Something can happen in our lives that precipitates a need to rethink our ordinary perspective. We are literally forced to reassess how we view life and adopt new paradigms of thought and action—or die trying.

It was the latter that happened to me. One sunny spring morning in late 1996, without warning, I launched my practice as a prayer-based spiritual healer, a Christian Science practitioner. A few years later, I was also ordained as an interfaith minister so that my healing and teaching ministry could better embrace all spiritual pathways.

This sudden change of career direction was certainly not anticipated. The day before that sunny morning, my life had been moving along pretty normally. Running my own company and presenting seminars and giving talks on ethics in business was, for the most part, enjoyable. I knew someday I would move into the more fulfilling work of individual mentoring and healing—something that had always come naturally to me. But not yet. Maybe when I was semi-retired and ready for a quieter life. Maybe when I possessed a more substantial and stable income to get all the children through school. Definitely not yet.

However—and here was the catch—a few months earlier I'd

made a deal with God. I remembered it well. For a while my life hadn't
been as happy or fulfilled as I would have liked and that low level
discomfort was starting to make itself felt. I remember thinking, surely
there is more to life than this. I began to wonder if I was really living.
Relationship issues, financial issues, minor health issues were getting
in the way—nothing bad, mostly just an awareness that I wasn't on
my right path. There existed a nagging feeling that there was something I was supposed to be doing with my life that I wasn't. I hadn't
a clue what. Trying to figure it out left me even more confused.

During that time in the early mornings before my workdays
started, I'd often wander along the beach near our home to think and
pray. This particular morning, I was sitting on a rock watching the
sun lazily haul itself over the horizon when I thought I saw a whale in
the distance. The Bible story of Jonah and the whale came to mind.
God wanted Jonah to go to Nineveh to preach but Jonah had other
ideas. Jonah had plenty of excuses each time God asked him to go.
Eventually, as the story goes, Jonah's disobedience got him into trouble
with God and a whale swallowed him whole. When he agreed to
implement God's plan the whale spat him onto dry land.

To me this story is allegorical. God does not punish us for mis-
behaving or disobeying. God is a power of Love that only knows us
as she created us—as spiritual and perfect beings always held in complete harmony. We punish ourselves by not following the divine guidance that continues to awaken us from the dream of mortality to this
spiritual identity. I'll explain this in more depth later but for the
moment it may help you to understand why I suddenly saw that I
was pulling a Jonah on God. I was simply not following the higher
guidance that was coming to me.

I saw that for many years I had felt I was not doing what God
wanted me to do—that there was a higher purpose for me—something I would love to do—that I was putting on hold due to the perceived necessity of meeting my financial commitments. The sense of
discomfort I had been feeling increasingly reminded me that perhaps
it was time I discovered what motivated me. Then perhaps I wouldn't
keep feeling I was being swallowed by whales.

Although I believe that God knows me only as she has created me—as a spiritual, perfect being—I still like to talk to her. Talking to God helps me feel the sense of God as All Love, as my loving, nurturing spiritual Father-Mother. Feeling immersed in this sense of loving care, I have come to trust that I will hear the guidance that harmonizes this human experience even as it lifts me out of the dream and back into my higher selfhood. Feeling encompassed in this sense of spiritual love and harmony is what heals: because our thought is filled with an expectation of good, our human experience manifests what we hold in thought. Trying to rationalize this whole dream experience and understand it logically, particularly in its relationship to spiritual reality, is impossible. Human reasoning just won't make sense of any of this. So I talk to God to come into my higher selfhood, my love consciousness.

Sitting on the rock that morning beside the sea, I made a deal with God. "Tell me," I said to God, "what it is you want me to do. I know you've probably told me hundreds of times but I will try harder not to block your message with my own will, my own ego fears and limitations. What you want me to do will in the end be what I love to do most. If you just make it really clear to me what it is you want me to do, I promise to be obedient."

My promises are never made lightly, so this was a big commitment for me. I needed to trust that through a sense of inspiration or my higher knowing, I would hear clearly what would give me the greatest fulfillment in my life and bring me back to a full understanding of my true identity as a spiritual expression of Love.

Soon I forgot about the deal—my promise to God—and continued on with my seminar and speaking engagements, and retained the low level discomfort. Then, a few months later, on that sunny spring morning, the sudden change of direction in my life happened. I woke up and knew it was time to become a fulltime healer and life guide. Not sometime in the future. Right then. This same clear message had come to me a number of times over the previous year but I had always dismissed it as ridiculous given all the practical reasons I thought I had to keep doing what I was doing. My well-planned life had continued.

This particular morning I tried again to dismiss the idea that had come to me. But it didn't work. The message was so clear I knew there was no choice but to obey. I recalled the deal I'd made with God those few months earlier and knew deep inside that even if I had no clue how such a dramatic change in my life could be accomplished, I could certainly trust that everything was unfolding exactly as it should.

So that day, without warning to anyone (including myself), I simply closed down my business and walked into a new adventure, one that had no signposts.

I wondered how I would survive such a quiet life. Later, I wondered how I ever thought spiritual healing and life guidance could be quiet. After the first months of settling into my practice, it had become anything but. Obviously God's plan didn't include quiet, boring or even stoic work. Doing his work embraces the joy, fulfillment and freedom that are part of divine Love's being.

I soon found that the majority of clients who came to me were doing exactly what I was doing—searching for an ever-deepening understanding of their spiritual identities. They were yearning to understand their identity. What could be more exhilarating than working with people who have grasped the most fulfilling, joyfilled— and at times frightening and confusing—thing they could do with their lives? These individuals had an insatiable desire to better understand how to live with others in harmony, in the Oneness of all creation.

Yes, this was definitely the work that God had given me to do— to awaken others to their innate joy and freedom, to help them come into their true awareness, while at the same time allowing me to do the same for myself. I realized I had loved lifting people up most of my life but now I saw the time for this healing and life guidance ministry to become my career had arrived. I could clearly see where my passion, purpose and career intersected.

The last few years have been for me a time of spectacular transformation in my life. They have been a time of discovery, allowing me to learn and demonstrate through active living, the truths I have been learning and teaching in the first half of my life—particularly about the power of unconditional love. On the surface, these years have appeared to others as one great upheaval that included the end of a long-term marriage and relocation half way around the world.

Years of non-stop busyness and worldly success have been followed by a period of feeling almost completely cut off from the rest of the world as I have taken time out to re-design my life to be something that feels truly authentic to me. Despite all the unaccustomed aloneness and anonymity, right from the outset I have felt that I was finally and fully alive. What a paradox! I have had to learn to live in the moment without trying to outline how the events in my life should unfold. I really have no idea what comes next. All I know is that every step of the adventure has been unfolding in perfect timing, and I have felt wonderfully cared for by the Universe. I have gained a delightful and ever increasing sense of lightness, freedom, joy and peace as I have learned to let go of any need to control, as I have learned to simply *live love*.

Just before I emigrated from New Zealand to the USA in 2001, a woman overheard me tell a friend that I had no clue why I was shifting countries. She told me I had been called to teach more people how to really live, rather than just talk about, the greater spiritual awareness they were discovering. Her comments have proven true. How fascinating, as she had never met me and knew nothing at all about my work.

Life is a magnificent journey once we let go of trying to orchestrate how we think it should look, and begin instead to *feel*, to trust and live Love's cosmic vision for us.

Re-designing Lives

As I said in the Introduction, there are many great books being written about profound spiritual insights that lead us towards knowing who we truly are and what we are here to do. There is, however, less written about the actual day-to-day practice of these insights.

My unique contribution to this body of literature concerns the practical application of such day-to-day spiritual healing in all the arenas of our lives as we continue to discover more about our authentic identity and purpose. This is what I help my clients achieve. I call this work of inner transformation or attaining true awareness "re-designing lives."

In my healing and life guidance practice I help clients re-design their lives by aiding them in breaking out of old ways that no longer serve them. They discover—rediscover—the joy and fulfillment that come from knowing themselves as perfect spiritual expressions of divine Love, never separate from their infinite Source. Witnessing ourselves in this way, we begin to see that by understanding our spiritual identity, we can write the script for this so-called human experience any way we choose.

There are many techniques such as creative visualization and various mind-over-matter formulas that sound similar, but are actually quite different. I'll go into more detail later, but for now the basic difference is that when we understand ultimate reality as solely spiritual, not physical, we come to see that when we hold thoughts of harmony and love—of joy, freedom and peace—these thoughts manifest in the "things" that represent these qualities. Our human lives simply pattern what we are holding in consciousness. When we understand that our Father-Mother Love is always beholding us as she created us, in utter loveliness, then we trust that our needs will always be abundantly met. Knowing this, we write beautiful scripts for ourselves without ever needing to outline how our lives are supposed to look. What adventure!

I also help my clients remember how to live in open-hearted love, in their natural *love consciousness* that has no blocks or limits. Such learning literally transforms lives by healing, by obliterating anything that limits or diminishes the beauty, the joy, freedom and peace that are natural to spiritual beings.

Clients come to me seeking healing through prayer for difficulties at home or at work, in a relationship, perhaps for a drug or alcohol related problem or for the healing of some other addiction. I work with clients seeking physical healing of some illness or disease. Some come as a last resort after medical or alternative healing methods have failed. Others, who have always relied on metaphysical healing, come knowing there is nothing that is too difficult to be healed through prayer. They simply need some help to break the illusion in which they seem trapped. Almost without exception, my clients acknowledge the power of prayer and the role of the one Mind, God, connecting the Universe.

These spiritual seekers, like me, seem to feel a growing urgency to break out of a way of life that feels as if it's strangling them. As we start to explore together the ideas I've written about in this book, it is as if we can breathe again for the first time in years. Often a sense of childlike joy and wonder about spiritual things takes over—an urge to get up and dance and sing in release and relief. We remember life is a journey of discovery and adventure, a journey to Love. And we accept that, on the journey, it is okay to make mistakes, to think differently, to laugh and cry, get things right sometimes, mess up other times. We learn that it takes a whole lot of courage to listen to our hearts and follow that still small voice within. But all of this process, this journeying, is okay.

I have written this book, *Living Love*, at the urging of clients, to support their spiritual journeys, and also to support the journeys of all spiritual seekers looking for new ways to do life. Every one of you can make this journey, discover these truths for yourself, learn to heal, learn to transform or re-design your lives. Every one of you can do this for yourself if you are ready and willing to step out of the old ways. I know. I am on the same journey.

The ideas in this book are based on my learning and experiences. You can explore the results of my journey, but ultimately it will be *your* own inner knowing—or true awareness—and day-to-day experiences that will lead you to find the truth or otherwise of what I share.

CHAPTER 4

WHAT I'VE LEARNED ALONG THE WAY

Divine Love always has met, and always will meet, every human need.
Mary Baker Eddy

S O WHAT HAS MY JOURNEY TO TRUTH TAUGHT ME? WHAT DO I know? I know that for all of us, living love, being love, all love, is what we're aiming for. Much of the time we appear to miss the mark.

The original definition of the old theological word "sin" was "to miss the mark." It was an archery term meaning to miss the bull's eye, the center. Understood this way, "sin" seems such a forgiving word compared to the negative emotional and judgmental connotations it has come to possess within the Christian church in particular. *A Course in Miracles* defines sin as lack of love, a mistake to be corrected rather than an evil to be punished.

I know for certain that we are not stuck with scarcity and lack, particularly lack of love and harmony. With practice and persistence we miss the mark less often. Then our lives are transformed—our hearts sing, our eyes light up. There is less fear, less anger, more peace and safety. We feel more and more *alive*. Life becomes a game. We and everything and everybody we touch become the winners.

Seeing through the eyes of Love, the eyes of God, is our natural, eternal state even if we have forgotten this fact and believe it will take an endlessly long time to achieve. We are *already* at the point of perfection and it is this knowing, even just in occasional glimpses, which heals instantly.

A few years ago I was invited by a prison counselor, Mike, to take part in a two hour rehabilitation session with a group of twelve inmates, mostly young men in their twenties and thirties. When we walked into the room the atmosphere was nothing less than hostile. Not only was the hostility directed at the two of us but it shot between the young men as well.

Mike started off talking to them about his life on the streets and about being in prison numerous times for violent and drug related crimes. He then went on to talk about his present life not only as a counselor but also as the owner of a successful building construction company. He spoke of the turnaround in his life when he realized that he could take control of his living and be someone he could at least like, if not love. He also saw that everyone has within them a heart of love—a spiritual center—and when they find how to reach this core, good things happen with increasing frequency. All the fear, anger and violence is replaced by an almost overwhelming need to reach out and lift other people up. Mike had started his construction company to give employment to people just released from prison.

Up to this point in Mike's talk, the inmates had been fidgeting and grumbling about how some people get all the luck. But they appeared to be listening and when Mike asked everyone to stand up and face a partner they did so hesitantly. The request to "look into your partner's eyes and don't take your eyes off them until I say so," was met with anger. The response, "What a stupid thing to ask," masked the hidden fear of being vulnerable to another person. There was almost a riot on the spot but Mike, an ex-con, was not to be taken lightly. Soon the anger turned to resentful muttering, although at least five minutes passed before everyone was able to keep their eyes focused on their partner and the room quieted.

My partner, a tough, tattooed Polynesian man of about thirty, settled reluctantly and defiantly into my gaze. I soon noticed he had the most beautiful deep brown eyes, and before long I felt I was swimming in them. Some people say the eyes are the window to the soul. I felt a deep sense of peace and love welling up within me, and I started to wonder, who was this person behind the mask of hostility and . . .

was it fear?

After awhile, maybe another five minutes, the eyes that had seemed so hostile seemed to be laughing gently. When I whispered to him that he had the most beautiful eyes I'd ever seen, he put his strong arms round me with such tenderness, and started to cry quietly. It seemed his whole beautiful soul was once more being set free.

When we were eventually invited to sit down there was the gentlest sense of release and healing in the room. We all talked quietly about what had happened, even the few who had resisted most strongly letting their walls down. And finally the discussion turned to how the group could work together as a team, perhaps forming their own building site clearing crew when they were eventually released.

I wonder what has happened to these young men since that encounter? I know what happened to me. I was blessed with further healing of prejudice and judgment and I saw love where defensiveness and hardness had seemed to be.

As I said earlier, seeing through the eyes of Love is our natural, spiritual state, reflected in our human lives. It's not a process of learning. It's not really even a journey. Seeing through the eyes of Love is waking to remember our *present spiritual perfection*, that which always has been and always will be. It is waking from the dream state of this human experience to know that there are not two states of being. There is only the one spiritual and perfect state of joy and freedom.

Now is certainly time to wake up, and this is what I call the (r)evolution (a revolution and an evolution) of consciousness happening on the planet.

I know from my healing practice how many people are a part of this awakening and not just through one or two spiritual practices and religions. Many traditions accept these truths, at least in part, and many individuals I know are discovering these truths entirely by themselves.

While people from many religious traditions talk of the ancient mystics and prophets, every one of us has the potential to be a mystic or prophet. We all have a direct path to our Father-Mother God through our own love consciousness. None of us needs an intermediary except perhaps to help us get started. Truth, God, Love, whatever you want to call it, is universal. Truth is nameless, beyond being named, for it transcends the boundaries of language. There are as many ways to speak of this God concept as there are people in this universe.

The effects of this (r)evolution of consciousness will become more and more apparent both as fear, hatred and anger lose their stranglehold and as we discover a different way of being together. Author Gary Zukav says there is a new species being born within us— multi-sensory beings (rather than five sensory beings) who are learning to live with authentic power rather than through external power. Authentic power involves creating such a reverence for life in all its forms—including each other—that we value and feel safe with diversity. We are able to focus on discovering and living our purpose in this life rather than worrying about and trying to control how others are living their lives.

Striving to manipulate and control our circumstances, or in fact anything external to us, including other people, is the pursuit of external power, the old way of being together. External power no longer works. Authentic power is not competitive or controlling but enables cooperation and sharing. It is about living love in harmony with others and our world.

I know from my spiritual practice that many of the people reading this, who have not yet articulated their eternal awareness, will be saying, "I know this! I've always known these truths deep down inside. I just couldn't consciously bring them forth."

CHAPTER 5

HOW I GIVE HEALING TREATMENTS

In the life God has in mind for us we grow more and more beautiful and know more and more joy.
Marianne Williamson

THERE ARE MANY WAYS TO GIVE EFFECTIVE HEALING TREATMENTS or affirmations, and each of you knows, or will find out, what works best for you. Some people amaze me with their ability to sit still in deep contemplation for hours. I'm hopeless at this. I wriggle and squirm, my thoughts wandering in all directions. The particular way in which we pray or meditate does not matter. Whatever our unique qualities are, there is always a way to pray that will work effectively for us. When I had little children around me all day, I found I could pray "on the run." The important point when learning to pray is to understand that any kind of talking to God is effective in seeing though the illusion of discord and limitation in our lives.

For some years now my favorite way to give a healing treatment—it keeps me happily in one place—is to curl up with my laptop on my knee and talk to God. I type, "Dear Father-Mother God (or Love, or whatever I'm calling God that day), what do I need to know?"—or something to that effect. When I do this, I remember I am accessing the spiritual knowing that is part of my love consciousness—bringing my thoughts into line with what God, divine Love, already knows.

When I talk to God like this I am moving beyond the supposed limited ego consciousness. I am remembering I do not have two separate minds, a lower mind and a higher mind, but just the one Mind, infinite wisdom that is God. Some traditions call this the Christ Truth coming to the human consciousness, some call it angel thoughts, some, spirit guides. These are some of the various ways we choose to describe our oneness in Love, our here-and-now state of spiritual knowing.

[Note: When I use the word "Christ" I am not referring to the man, Jesus, but to the Christ consciousness or Truth consciousness, the spiritual knowing which Jesus possessed, which we all possess as spiritual expressions of God.]

So, as I listen for what love or my higher consciousness is saying, I simply type whatever comes to my thought. I love what I hear—never dull or repetitive, but so fresh and inspired. Often I share what I've written with my clients and many times they say something to the effect, "I didn't tell you that. I'd forgotten. How did you know that was the underlying problem that needed releasing?"

I remember once being asked to pray for a man who had a chronic sore throat. As I listened, it became clear that I needed to see he was not subject to bouts of anger and criticism directed at his children. I didn't know this man—I didn't even know he had children—so there was no logical reason for me to think this. However, I trusted this inspiration and prayed to see that this man, as a divine spiritual being, could not possess any qualities that were not beautiful and Godlike. When he called the next day to say he was feeling much better, he mentioned that when he came home from work the previous evening, he'd felt such a sense of unaccustomed peace and calm and had enjoyed playing with his children, something he had not done for some years. I told this man of my insight that as a child of God he could not be subject to bouts of anger and criticism of his children. He immediately recognized this was the underlying issue that had needed healing, although he had not been conscious of this until that moment.

The Christ Truth comes to consciousness uncovering whatever needs adjusting and showing us what God already knows.

What doesn't the one infinite, eternal Mind know? Just as rays of sunlight are the *evidence* or manifestation of the sun, so are we the evidence of the one Mind, Eternal Knowing, Infinite Wisdom. Without the sun the rays could not exist, yet the sunbeams point to the sun's existence. Even if clouds cover our perception of the sun, we know the sunbeams and the sun still exist. We know everything there is to know—although we may have forgotten this in our human experience.

Throughout this book, mostly at the end of the chapters, boxed and in italics, are some of the treatments I have given over the last few years. I present them here mostly in the first person, should you want to use them for your own personal prayers or affirmations. I hope also that they may help you see different possibilities for your own healing work for yourself and others. There are no formulas, no processes to be followed. You will find your own creative ways to get to the *feeling* of love and harmony as your natural state of being—to know there is no separation in the oneness of Love, of which you are an essential, indispensable part.

CHAPTER 6

ABOUT WRITING LIVING LOVE

Work is love made manifest.
                    Kahlil Gibran

I HAVE CALLED THIS BOOK *LIVING LOVE* BECAUSE THE KEY TO EF-
fective healing in our lives, and the key to discovering our true
identity and purpose, is in living each day what we are learning about
our oneness with the power of divine Love. To live in the heart of divine
Love day-by-day is what we're aiming for. *Living love*, when spiritually understood and practiced, is an ever-expanding feeling of joy,
freedom, peace and inner fulfillment—of being who we already are
and of doing what we came here to do, NOW. Even if we only manage to fully live love a little of the time, the feeling is deeply satisfying.

Living as much as we are able in this state of harmony and love
does not mean that the shadow side of human experience—the fears,
doubts and frustrations that seem to be part of living out this particular stage of experience—won't surface. The clouds will roll in, but
the more we choose to see we are not subject to external forces like
heredity or chance, that we're not simply pawns in some cosmic game,
the more we will see that the adventure and challenge of this experience is within our control. And on our darker days we can remember
the sun still shines and the sunbeams are still the perfect emanations
of the sun. As the light emerges, we will see these shadow experiences
as opportunities to push higher in the understanding of our true spiri-

tual selfhood. We see we are writing our own scripts. And for me at least, I know that without these opportunities to push higher and rise above the clouds, I would probably settle for the status quo, some kind of just-average existence that lets me stay within known boundaries. My motivation to push forward would simply not be there without these discomforts to drive me!

Thus, the more we grow into and live at ease within a heart-based state of love consciousness, the more naturally we find we can heal, dispose of, anything that no longer serves us in this experience. Although we may learn great lessons from the challenges we face in our day-to-day lives, I do not believe we have to accept any permanence about any of these challenges, any of the doubts, fears and problems that confront us. Yes, we need to pay attention to the lessons they teach us. They show us where we want to make changes in our lives, how to move forward more effectively, but once we learn the lessons, we simply grow beyond these challenges and are rid of them.

In the following pages, I will show the extent of what is possible in creating lives that are lived from a love-centered model when we learn how to heal effectively and consistently.

Surprising as it may seem to some of you, there are already many healers on the planet who know exactly what I am talking about here. For thousands of years there have been mystics and prophets teaching these concepts, each from unique and varied visions and experiences. More recently, over the last 125 years or so, healing as I talk about here has been part of the Christian Science tradition, as well as in some of the New Thought teachings. More recently still, many of the new spiritual teachings and traditional churches have embraced healing through prayer, at least to some extent.

Am I producing something new? No. I am simply articulating what we have all inherently known but may have forgotten in this dulling sleep state we have been lost in for so long. But these ideas are new in the sense they are based on my own vision and unique experience. Throughout the book I mostly refer to "we" because learning to live love (not just talk about it) is still very much my journey too. We are all moving forward together.

I trust you will find fresh perspectives here to add to and enhance your own vision, just as I will learn from yours when you are ready to share with me.

A promise of perfect living and perfect loving

Within me is a gentle softness, a sweetness so beautiful, a preciousness that is my true self. This self welcomes all joy, love and intimacy into my life now with no blocks of fear, hurt, tension, or disillusionment over past experiences. My perfect self opens with childlike innocence and trust to the promise of perfect living. Effortlessly I radiate laughter, spontaneity, boundless joy and loving back out to the Universe, drawing to me all the wonder and abundant fulfillment of a truly creative life of love.

This self does not glory in suffering, does not struggle up to perfection or perfect knowing, does not become embittered by life and shut off from love offered, but laughs in the face of adversity and determines more than ever to break through the clouds above. I open myself to moment by moment acceptance of all the ways divine Love is pouring into my conscious experience glorious opportunities to experience perfect beauty, exhilaration, exquisite joy and intimacy, tender peace and gentle flowing. I open to the ever-unfolding promise of heaven on earth. I open, not to something out there on a higher level of consciousness, but to ever present, here and now magnificence in this human experience just as I am NOW.

I watch in awesome peace and stillness as the exquisite images I have allowed into my consciousness evidence in my life. The dreams I once more dare to dream fulfill themselves beyond my wildest imaginations. There are no limits as I let go.

PART TWO

UNDERSTANDING LOVE:

FEELING LOVE

CHAPTER 7

FROM DESCRIBING LOVE TO FEELING LOVE:

THE ESSENTIAL TASK

In him to whom love dwells the whole world is but one family.
Gautama Buddha

THIS CHAPTER COULD BE CALLED *A FUTILE ATTEMPT TO DE-fine and Describe Love.* I mean, what more can be said about love? Mankind has been preoccupied with trying to define and describe love for centuries. Love is the subject of some of the most exquisite poetry, prose, dance, art, theater and music ever composed.

While some languages have various words that describe different degrees of love, English only uses "love." My sense is that adequately defining or describing love in words is impossible simply because love is a *feeling*. When we trust what our heart and soul convey to us through feelings, we come to know what love means, or at least what our concept of love is. At its height, love might feel like the sheer ecstasy that pours over us when we read exquisite poetry or are ardently in love, or it might simply be the sense of mild pleasure felt sitting in the sun on a warm day. We can love ice cream, we can love flowers or cars, horses or painting, or music. We can love our neighbor, we can love our children, we can love our life partner, we can love God. We know clearly that there are different degrees of love, everything from physical attraction, self-love, romantic love, love of specific actions and objects, to a kind of transcendent love, a passion that somehow defies all human boundaries and transcends all human description.

In his book, *How To Know God*, Deepak Chopra says that in the early stages of spiritual growth, the "force field of love" is weak as we struggle with doubt and fear, anger, jealousy, judgment, and all the other conflicting emotions that block our perception of love. Chopra notes that it takes years of clearing these inner blockages before we realize how immensely powerful God's force is, and that nothing will pull us away from it. Our perception of love changes from a personal emotion to a cosmic energy. When this happens we no longer see God as a separate object to love but we become one with love.

I agree it may—though not necessarily—take years or lifetimes even to reach anything like a consistent level of such spiritual knowing, a level where ultimately a physical or bodily state of being no longer serves us and we simply move into a purely spiritual state of being. However, I also know from my own healing work that even a small glimpse or recollection of our true oneness with Love is enough to awaken us, at least temporarily, from this limited mortal dream-state and allow healing to occur, often instantaneously. We may not see clearly enough yet to move beyond the human experience permanently, but there is plenty we can do in the meantime to transform our love into something increasingly spectacular.

Even if just for a few moments I feel immersed in and surrounded by Love, I can feel that my clients are also one with this Love. There is just love everywhere. There is no place for inharmony, sickness, sadness, confusion or any other type of limitation in this kind of knowing. These restrictions are simply part of the dream that there is something besides the one power of divine Spirit. There is not. *Feeling* the allness of Love is the healing. Because there are no barriers of time or space to the allness of Love, it makes no difference to healing whether my client is beside me or on the other side of the planet.

I also know that relative newcomers to this understanding of Love are able to heal when they glimpse these ideas. In fact, little children can often heal with little spiritual learning. What they lack in spiritual teaching, they make up for in their innate loving kindness, their purity and innocence of thought, and sometimes in an inherent spiritual knowing that transcends anything they might have been taught. Because little children haven't yet learned to question and doubt, they can often accept spiritual truths far more readily than their elders.

My oldest son, Craden, was barely two years old and just starting to string sentences together when I became very ill with mumps. Despite my own efforts and the efforts of a Christian Science practitioner, a spiritual healer, my physical condition continued to worsen. At the time I was feeling overwhelmed and exhausted nursing a new baby while trying to be the perfect wife and mother. When, after several days, the healing wasn't forthcoming, my husband called in a local doctor who promptly told me that I should be in a hospital where I could be properly cared for. He expected I would probably need to be there for at least two weeks. I was horrified at the thought of being separated from my family and asked him if we could wait until the next day to see if I was better. While he laughed at what obviously sounded completely improbable to him, he also knew of my reliance on metaphysical healing and agreed to one more night at home.

I lay in bed feeling wretched. I looked awful. I couldn't do anything. I couldn't even heal this illness. What was the point of one more night? I felt as if I was useless. I felt very sorry for myself. Suddenly Craden stomped into the room wearing his new, but now muddy, black rain boots. I couldn't even muster up the energy to scold him. He stopped, gazed at me long and hard, then announced very matter-of-factly, "God loves you"—and stomped back out of the room.

I was so surprised I just lay there not knowing what to think. But then the truth and power of what he'd said hit me. Of course God loved me. And if God loved me how could I possibly be anything but lovely? This little boy at two knew enough to know that God loved me, and that meant I didn't need to be sad, sorry or sick.

There didn't seem much point lying there any longer so I got up, dressed, and wandered out into the garden where my husband was still talking to the doctor. The sight of me up and the swelling going down fast was almost too much for the doctor. I guess he'd never seen an instantaneous healing. He just shook his head in bewilderment and left. I couldn't help laughing in joy and gratitude.

I learned so much that day about trust and innocence. I remembered that healing is simple—simple but not easy, at least not for those of us who make it complicated and refuse to trust. That day I learned a whole lot more about the healing power of love.

We can only know love as we *feel* love. Without feeling love we are at a loss to describe it. Almost indescribable in words, love is a feeling that comes to reside deep within our soul. Cosmic, spiritual love is far beyond and above a temporary physical emotion. We simply come to know this feeling. We see it evidenced in a smile, in a baby's delighted chortle, in an awe-inspiring sunrise or sunset. We feel it in a hug, in the warmth of the sunshine and the cool of a rain shower. We glimpse it in whatever brings us utter delight and gentle peace.

I know from my own experience how an understanding, even just a fledgling understanding of the power of Love, as in the case of this two year old child, can literally transform and heal lives.

At the end of the day, healing is not about a process of getting from A to Z, or of self-improvement and mastery. It is about waking up to glimpse our present perfection as a spiritual expression of divine Love. The words are not the key. What matters above all else is the *feeling* of living love, and the awareness that there is just love. Nothing else.

Effortless unfolding

What is the truth about me at this moment? I am spiritual, perfect, complete and in full joy and harmony right at this moment and forever. What appears to be happening in the human scene is simply the outcome of my human thinking at this time. At any moment I can change the script to one of perfect harmony and fulfillment.

I do not need to expect delays to the evidence of perfect harmony and joy. I do not need to learn something in order to be better and happier. Right now I am at the point of perfection and as I awaken to this understanding of what is already true, the evidence appears instantly.

Discord, frustration, loneliness, fear, tension and all the other seeming beliefs of mortality have no reality and no law to support them. All law is divine, eternal, purely spiritual and therefore all good. These false beliefs also have no substance because all substance is divine, eternal, purely spiritual and therefore all good. There is no power to support the lie of mortality and materiality, and I am not subject to powerless nothingness. I am not vulnerable to what other people think or say or do, nor are there any circumstances that are outside my control or influence. The dream of human existence is simply that, a dream.

Right in this moment and forever I am able to know only what is true —my God-given spiritual perfection, harmony, fulfillment, joy, peace, wisdom, appreciation, satisfaction. With this knowledge I am able to let go of the lie and happily watch harmony effortlessly and beautifully unfold in my life, moment by moment by moment.

CHAPTER 8

DO YOU KNOW HOW MUCH GOD LOVES YOU?

God is love; and he that dwelleth in love
dwelleth in God and God in him

The Gospel of St John

To understand love more deeply and therefore to understand how to live love more fully, we must recognize our relationship to the one Source of all creation, God. Knowing that God is divine Love itself, it stands to reason that our relationship with God must be one of unconditional and infinite love. There can be no separation between creator and creation. God is Love and knows only love. Therefore whatever Love creates must be loving. We are One with, and in, Love. We can each say, "I am love." Who is this 'I?' Our spiritual self that is One with God, or created by God, Love.

How does understanding our real spiritual relationship to God help us in the present moment when we seem to be lost in the dream of a limited and often discordant human selfhood? Even a small glimpse of the truth of our true spiritual and perfect union with God prompts us to remember our identity. Just this small glimpse helps us rise somewhat out of this dream state of physical limitation. As we remember who we really are, the dream of limitation and discord starts to lose its hold over us and progressively we gain a greater sense of joy, freedom and peace—we are able to feel a deeper sense of our Father-Mother God's love for us.

A gentle sense of safety and security helps us feel increasingly loved and loving, even though God does not know anything about our limitations in this world of physical form. As we move ever closer to understanding the Oneness, the Allness of the power of divine Love, our human lives continue to reflect our expanding awareness of what is really true. Our lives become more and more harmonious—even spectacular.

Thinking of God as our Father-Mother who cares for and protects us is a step in the right direction towards understanding more about love. Better still is *feeling* this sense of harmony and peace that brings us into balance with the truth of who we are. The activities and events of our human lives then adjust themselves to mirror this harmony.

The remainder of this chapter was originally written to a young client who needed help *feeling* how much he is truly loved by his Father-Mother God. I met Paul when I was giving a talk to a group of college students about the power of unconditional love and acceptance. I noticed tears running down Paul's face and, when he talked to me later, he said he'd made such a mess of his life he really felt there was nothing he could do to regain the trust and forgiveness of either his parents or God.

There was of course plenty he could do, I assured him, but he first needed to gain his own trust and forgiveness. That meant first learning to love himself just as he was. We all make so-called mistakes but even these mistakes are actually our best sense of right at the time. Paul and I worked together over a few weeks until I felt sure he was once more reconnected to love. He now has a great relationship with his parents and he feels connected strongly to God, his unfailing source. He has recently become a healer.

The following message, originally written to Paul, can be helpful for all of us.

Do you know how much God loves you?

God loves you so much that nothing can truly describe the completeness and the infinite nature of this unconditional love. Right now you dwell in the atmosphere of divine Love and you can never exist outside this Love. Nothing you can ever do or say will stop him loving you. It doesn't matter if you've done things that you are convinced are reason for him to give up on you, he hasn't.

How can this be? Because he sees you as he made you—loving, lovable, loved. In the first chapter of the Bible it says, "And God saw everything that he had made and behold it was very good." That includes you!

What about the bad things you associate with yourself? What about the second chapter of Genesis where Adam and Eve supposedly messed things up? What if you think of yourself as a sinner who has fallen from grace, perhaps bound for hell?

Many years ago I met Jason, a young man who was in all sorts of trouble. Although he was a top student, he and his peer group had become involved in drugs. Eventually, he dropped out of school. His parents were so angry with him they refused to have him in the house until he sorted himself out. To make matters worse, he had been arrested for the possession and sale of drugs and was about to be tried in court. A prison sentence was inevitable given the train of events. He felt completely trapped with no way out.

But there is always a way out. It is never too late. A friend suggested he look for a spiritual solution, which he did. As this young man started to learn about his relationship with his Father-Mother God, infinite Love, he began to see events in a different light. He realized that his destructive behavior was preventing him from feeling the all power of God's love. In the same way that Jason wouldn't feel the sun's abundant warmth by sitting in a room with the curtains closed, so too he was making the conscious decision to shut himself away from the warmth and comfort of divine Love by thinking and acting in ways that hurt him and others. The sun was still out there shining but he began to realize he was going to have to open the curtains.

He set out to learn all he could about his spiritual selfhood. He was drawn to the idea in the first chapter of the Bible that man is made in the image of God. As the image of God, he must possess the perfection that God embodies. He saw the Adam and Eve story in the second chapter of the Bible as simply an allegory attempting to explain why humankind appears to have fallen into a deep sleep, dreaming that we are limited, discordant mortals. Jason saw he had a choice to make. Either he could choose to wake up and move out of this dream, or he could remain fast asleep. He also came to see that heaven and hell are not places, but simply states of thought. He liked the idea in Mary Baker Eddy's book, *Science and Health*, that sin makes its own hell, and goodness its own heaven. He also discovered that the original meaning of the word "sin" has its roots in an archery term meaning "to miss the mark." He realized that sin might be seen as thinking and behavior that misses the mark—that hurts oneself or others.

If we don't want to make life hell for ourselves, we have to ensure that our thoughts and actions are reflecting our spiritual selfhood, that our thoughts are loving and kind. Selfishness, anger, lying, and cheating, all eventually create a hellish misery, although if they are concepts we've lived with throughout our lives they may be all we really know—our defense or survival mechanisms. Because these limiting concepts are not expressions of love they separate us from the all-powerful source of all good, divine Love, God, by blocking our ability to feel this goodness. These limiting concepts are the curtains drawn across the window. Conversely, we create our own heaven when our thoughts, and therefore our experience, is filled with love and harmony.

These concepts taught Jason powerful lessons and helped him understand that while the choices we make are always our highest sense of right in any moment (and of course we may change our mind in the very next moment), we can make choices that lead to truly fulfilling and happy lives.

And this is what happened to Jason. As his thought filled with the understanding of his present perfection as a child of God, his desire to lead the sort of life he had been living disappeared. He started to help at-risk young kids and went back to school and to his family. His addiction to drugs was completely healed. By the time the trial came around the judge commented on this complete transformation and just sentenced him to community service, enabling him to continue helping at-risk kids.

We create our own heaven or our own hell. Once we know this then the choice is ours. A God that is All Love is not punishing us, and we certainly don't want to be punishing ourselves. How often people, young and old, can feel they've "burned their bridges" or that the damage is done and there's no way out.

There is always a way out when we remember that we are one with our Source, never separate from God who has created us perfect in his image. There is always a way out when we realize we can choose to be the way God has made us, to live love as part of our true God-like, spiritual identity. When we remember how much God loves us we are once more able to be the lovable pure expression of love God sees.

If we accept that God is all there is and that God is the power of Love itself, then God can know only love—what is loving and lovable. As Love is the only power there is, how can there be anything that is not the pure and perfect expression of Love? Right now and always she sees each of her children as spiritual manifestations of her Love—perfect, complete, reflecting all the good that is. She loves us without any conditions. This is the Father-Motherhood of Love.

We sometimes see this love expressed by parents to their children. When my children were young and sometimes misbehaved I would tell them in no uncertain terms I didn't love their behavior but they needed to know there wasn't a thing in the world they could ever do that would stop me loving them. This helped them see their own spiritual beauty and goodness, and as they did so they naturally wanted to express their spiritual beauty in improved behavior. The fear that might have manifested as anger, jealousy, revenge, hurt feelings or resentment was replaced by a warm and comforting feeling of love and unconditional acceptance. They came home to their natural state of love consciousness.

We all need to feel love without conditions, and we can because this is exactly how God loves each of us. We can learn to love ourselves unconditionally too, getting beyond the fearful thought, "I am my behavior." I know from experience how difficult the challenge is for some of us to learn to love and accept ourselves just as we are.

It has taken me a long time to move from the logical understanding that I *should* love myself, to the intuitive feeling of self-acceptance and love in my heart. The family and social conditioning that judged my so-called inappropriate childhood behavior—emotional outbursts, irrational responses, selfishness, impatience—as "bad" did a splendid job of ensuring that, even in adulthood, I continued to think of myself as a bad person, or at least less than adequate. Only through a growing awareness of my identity as a spiritual expression of Love have I come to accept in my heart and soul that I am lovable *just as I am*. And now, for the first time since I was a little child I believe it when I am told I am loved just as I am. What a sense of freedom, joy and peace comes with this knowing. Wow!

I know you too can feel the power and bliss of this unconditional acceptance just as you are too.

I love the message in the movie *Bridget Jones' Diary* (a modern day version of Jane Austen's classic, *Pride and Prejudice*) which portrays the utter amazement that heroine Bridget feels when hero Darcy says he loves her just as she is. How could that be when she has behaved so badly? That anyone could love her just as she is is such a revelation to her, and slowly she settles into the warm satisfaction that she is lovable regardless of what she does. She also finds herself wanting to live more love, to be more loving— the natural outcome of experiencing love without conditions.

Every one of us makes mistakes, and some mistakes are more catastrophic than others. But some of the greatest progress we make in life comes from the lessons we learn from those mistakes. In a curious way we can ultimately win more than we lose from our mistakes. If you've learned the lesson, don't keep kicking yourself in the shins forever.

Again, remember God loves you just as you are. And remember too, we all do the greatest good because we love; we love to live in Love—not out of fear nor because we are told we should. We can learn to love ourselves as God loves us. When we glimpse even just a little of the magnitude of God's love for us we start to live in the warmth and glow of that security and wonder. Immersed in this love, we can't help loving. As we love effortlessly we discover and live our true identity—our purpose and vision.

A treatment for fear

Dear Father Mother God, right now you are holding this dear child in your arms, pouring in floodtides of gentle nurturing love; reminding him of what he has always known about his spiritual, eternal perfection as the very evidence of all that you are. Because divine Love is all that truly exists, Love's child naturally and effortlessly radiates this perfect harmony. He is able to feel safe and protected, knowing that even when the path ahead is hidden in the undergrowth he is always able to see the next step, and the next and the next, as he moves courageously forward into this unknown. He can never move outside Love's Allness because this Allness is his forever home.

Let go, Dear One, and feel the warm, safe presence of this atmosphere of Love surrounding and protecting you. You don't need to know what happens next. You only need to know that right now you are safe and very loved. And if you live each moment in this trust, the moments will unfold into days and weeks and years and you will see the intricate and beautiful design of your life. Your life has always been an adventure and it has had some unexpected turns, but you have never ever been forsaken and you never will be. It is okay to be frightened when you can't see your way in the dark. The dawn will always come and with it your strength and courage, your humor and joy. As you see the spectacular sunrise of this new and fresh awakening you will certainly remember and celebrate who you truly are.

Remember how much you are loved. Right now Love is wrapping you in a huge fluffy blanket of peace and light. You are very safe.

CHAPTER 9

LOVE WITHOUT JUDGMENT

My humanity is bound up in yours,
for we can only be human together.
Archbishop Desmond Tutu

ONCE WE BECOME AWARE OF THE MAGNITUDE AND WHOLENESS of God's eternal love for us—we begin to understand how our purpose is also to be found in this ocean of love. Our ultimate purpose is to be found in living love.

Because there is actually no possible separation from the oneness of Love, in which we each have our unique niche, we come to see that we can appreciate and love ourselves just as we are. There is no need to compare ourselves to others. Just as we know that the number ten is inherently no more or less important than the number three, there is no temptation to judge ourselves or others as better or worse, higher or lower, more or less. When we understand our perfection just as God has created us in his spiritual image and likeness, we are free to fully appreciate our uniqueness. This understanding naturally translates into daily living that is tolerant and accepting of the diversity that makes our lives on the planet so enchanting.

We simply cannot accept the oneness of Love, the oneness of all creation, and then leave ourselves out of it. We cannot love fully and at the same time judge ourselves or others as less than whole.

I have come to see that loving ourselves is vital because loving others unconditionally is actually impossible unless we first love ourselves. If we do not love ourselves and accept ourselves just as we are, we will put conditions on our love for others. What are they giving us in return? Are they appreciating what we're giving them? Do they make us feel better about ourselves? Do they boost our self-esteem? In other words, do we love others in order to be more loved, in order to get something we're simply not giving to ourselves? "Giving" in order to "get" is clearly not love *without* conditions. Giving for the purpose of receiving is an example of conditional love based on the fear that we can lack or be deprived of something we need. We have forgotten that in oneness all our needs will be abundantly met by divine Love even though we may not know how this will happen.

When someone is unkind to us, critical or judgmental of our efforts to reach out, we need to ask ourselves whether we love them regardless. Or do we withdraw with hurt feelings or self-righteous judgment, feeling they don't deserve what we're giving them? If so, we are expecting something in return.

And yet, is it not natural to expect something in return for our good deeds? Yes, it is very natural, and we usually teach our children to expect rewards for doing good. But this does not teach them to love without conditions. Do we love to do good because we get praise and adulation or because our true reward is simply the ever increasing warmth of love we feel in our own heart and soul when we pour out the overflow, the abundance of our own inner reserves of love. Pouring forth love with no expectation of anything in return can feel like the most selfish act possible because we gift so much good to ourselves in the process. Even as pouring forth love without expecting anything in return blesses all humanity, it also serves to increase the abundance of love, joy, vitality, warmth and delight within us. And this is the ultimate in finding true joy, freedom and peace through living love.

When we understand that love without conditions is the love of God, from which we are inseparable and of which we actually *are*, we so love ourselves—regardless of our idiosyncrasies—that this love overflows without judgment to everyone whose lives we touch. A heart already overflowing with love needs nothing but to continue its outpouring. Imagine a world where love pours forth freely like this, not because we think others lack what we have and not because we must heal someone or fix this world, but because there is so much love to share we simply cannot keep it all locked inside us.

The following was written for some high school seniors who were judging themselves—struggling with feelings of inadequacy, of not being good enough.

Loving Yourself Just As You Are

Jesus said the two greatest commandments are 1) that we love God and 2) that we love others as we love ourselves. We tend to notice the "love God" and""love others" commands more than the "*as* we love ourselves" command. Why are we taught that loving ourselves is selfish? When we truly love ourselves, the consciousness of love that fills us radiates out to others effortlessly.

Do you know how hard it is to love others, to be accepting, tolerant and non-judgmental, when we're critical, intolerant and judgmental of ourselves? Such judgmental thoughts lead us to compare ourselves to others—I'm not as good as… I'm not as smart, as beautiful, as handsome, as talented, as creative, as kind, as gentle, as lucky even. We often feel threatened by others' abilities and we try to pull them down in order to feel better about ourselves. She's cute but awfully egotistical. He's smart but he's a nerd. And with the person who really seems to have no faults—ah well, one day they'll fall on their face.

When you feel really good about who you are, no one feels like a threat to you and you're happy for people to be just the way they are wherever they are on their life path. Can't you see how hard it is to live in harmony, to expect to see the perfect child of God evidenced, when you're giving yourself and others such a difficult time?

We all make so-called mistakes in this human arena, we all mess up occasionally, even a whole lot. It's okay. Our mistakes don't make us bad people. Why not? Because at the time we made mistakes, these mistakes were actually our best sense of what was right—even if that moment was a fleeting moment of fear that manifested as anger, lack, retaliation or criticism. We all do the best we know how at any moment even if in the next moment we realize we made a poor choice.

When someone leads a life of extreme violence, hatred or cruelty, the likelihood is that they may not have known anything different in their own lives—this is the best they know how. They have probably never known what it feels like to truly love or be loved. Their lives exhibit a constant need to protect themselves from losing the things they think give them happiness and recognition. Terrorists and religious fanatics think the cause they stand for justifies annihilating others. However horrible this seems to those who think differently, the actions of these fanatics are nevertheless based on their highest sense of right at the time for gaining approval, fighting fear of disappointment and rejection from others, or even rejection from their god. Many British colonialists thought persecuting, or even annihilating "the infidel"—mostly people of indigenous cultures who wouldn't convert to Christianity—was the highest sense of right. Racial and religious prejudice still occurs today. A change of consciousness and perspective can certainly take time.

Bullying and teasing at school are attempts to gain acceptance by a peer group, motivated again by fear and a need to be loved and accepted. Refusal to willingly participate in household chores can be seen as laziness or selfishness but actually the choice at the time that seems our best sense of right might be a determination to put our own needs above those of others. As we grow in our understanding of the profound joy that comes from lighting up other people's lives and from sharing in cooperative community, we will naturally do things differently. In the meantime, our parents may find it necessary to force us to cooperate even with nothing more than a "do it because I say so" or a "don't be so selfish" reprimand. The old controls of shame and guilt may be the best they know how. In time they may discover that a more loving response of taking the time to discuss why living in harmony and community is important, and modeling this in their own lives, will bring mutual sharing and cooperation. We are all learning and growing and as we learn to love ourselves just as we are, we will naturally learn to love others just as they are.

The point is, why would we want to mess up our own lives deliberately by living in conflict with others? That's no fun. When we learn how a consciousness full of fear, hate and discord makes for an unhappy life, we will certainly not want that for ourselves.

As we start to understand how we create our own reality in this human drama according to what stems from our own consciousness, we'll want to create a life full of love and harmony. That means focusing our thoughts increasingly on what is loving and kind, on remembering the qualities that are natural to us as spiritual beings, qualities that are Godlike, loving and lovely. We'll see it doesn't make sense to get irritated and judgmental of others or ourselves, to say or even think things that are unkind and hurtful. We won't do things that harm others or ourselves because that would be writing a script for ourselves that would cause pain.

Again, this sounds simple but it isn't easy, not when we've spent a lifetime—lifetimes even—living the old paradigm of fear, hurt and judgment. While it takes a whole lot of patience to re-design our lives, we can gradually expand into this new way of living love as we become aware of the truth of who we are and what we are here to do.

Loving ourselves and others as the children of God means living in a way that honors and celebrates love. It means loving who we are, how we are, right where we are NOW. And when we do this, the stuff that no longer serves us will naturally drop away. We'll find what best serves not only our happiness but others' happiness as well. That's not selfish.

A friend once said to me that if she made "finding her bliss" (to quote Joseph Campbell) her highest priority, she'd spend every day soaking in a bubble bath reading magazines and sipping cool drinks. When she thought about this some more she realized she might do that for a very short time and then it would get boring and pointless. Her life experiences had taught her that what gives her the greatest joy is making a difference in other people's lives—and making a difference is a deep-down satisfaction that bubble baths just can't match. But she also realized that making a difference in her own life, discovering her true purpose, honoring her own dreams of what she wants to do with her life, and celebrating her own vision is a prerequisite to truly helping others. She is so right, and I haven't yet found someone who did not ultimately reach the same conclusion, even if through trial and error.

Following your dreams, discovering what you're passionate about doing, honoring your vision—yes, all these things are what make your heart sing and your eyes light up. When you live like this, not only do you love being who you are without judgment, condemnation or criticism, but also this unconditional love overflows to everyone around you. As your joy, freedom and peace extend to embrace others without judgment, you celebrate the extraordinary unity that exists in diversity. There is no separation—just oneness in Love.

Perfect Balance

Dear Father Mother, right now I am living your love. I am the pure and eternal spiritual expression of perfection. I am the manifestation, the evidence of divine Mind, the one all-knowing, infinitely wise and gentle Intelligence, God. I know all that I need to know. I can hear the Christ Truth guiding me into perfect good always. I am the evidence of Truth and Life and Principle. My life unfolds in perfect balance and perfect timing. There can be no over action, under action, reaction nor inaction—just perfect balance and perfect unfolding.

When I know this, my human experience evidences this perfection in joy, freedom and peace. There can be no discord, no overtiredness, no lack of rest, and no irritability. These lies have no power, no substance, no cause, and no law. There is nothing but pure goodness, divine energy in action, calmness. I do not need to struggle to be anything. I am already everything I need to be and when I let go of a sense of willpower and control, my life naturally evidences utter wonder and glory. Thank you Father Mother.

CHAPTER 10

FEELING LOVE REQUIRES PATIENCE

No heart has ever suffered when it goes in search of its dreams.
Paulo Coelho

A PRIME REQUISITE OF OUR SPIRITUAL JOURNEY IS PATIENCE. PAT-
ience and persistence in dropping the old ways of fear and
willpower are required to re-design our lives. Jesus' disciple, James,
tells us to "let patience have her perfect work." Just prior to saying
this James observes that we can rejoice when things are going badly!
Statements like this in the Bible used to really annoy me until I finally figured out what they meant.

Once we get a hint of the goal we're aiming for—in this case, to
live love, to live a life that is full of joy, freedom and peace—there's a
sense of urgency in reaching it. And yet we need a whole lot of patience. A goal like living love becomes a life goal as distinct from a
career goal like earning more money. Discovering how to live in love
is creating a whole new perspective on *how* we live and *who* we are.
Such discoveries take time. Working toward this goal requires discard-
ing old beliefs about "reality" and embracing new beliefs. It is a lifetime work—or more likely, lifetimes of work, as our changing perspective brings up all the heavy baggage in our lives that no longer
serves us.

But are we really willing to let go of these outdated thought-
models? It's hard to discard those old slippers that have served us well,
even when the toes are gone and the heels have worn through. It is

infinitely harder to discard the timeworn perceptions we've clung to as part of our identity for as long as we can remember. Sometimes adopting the willingness to soar free from the old control dramas—such as the need to control our own lives and the lives of those around us, or the need for security or affirmation— requires an unsolicited push. The list of the old stuff—the baggage—of doing life is endless, and yet all these perceptions around the need for external control must be let loose if we are to live more fully.

We need to be patient with ourselves (even rejoice when things go badly), and be patient with others who are trying to do the same. Fellow travelers, we all need support—not sabotage. It's not easy to change lifetimes of limited perceptions.

For instance, I've always protected myself by closing down or running away when I think I might get criticized. For me, being criticized means I might be rejected as inadequate or not good enough. I'm not someone who lashes out in anger. I don't yell and scream. I have always just become quiet and disappeared. Very often no one knows why. Imagine the misunderstandings that have never been healed. I simply have not taken risks when it comes to the possibility of getting hurt. Other people might use a different defense mechanism such as anger or retaliation. Either way, these mechanisms are all tools for avoidance, ways of dealing with the fear of potential loss of either love or control. When we're not living love, we're living with at least some degree of fear, and I've found my journey requires plenty of patience to change this pattern.

I've come to see that my protection mechanism of becoming quiet and running away no longer serves me. This control drama prevents meaningful dialogue and communication. If I can't say what I really think for fear of conflict or abandonment, my defense mechanism prevents me not only from getting to know myself but also from developing meaningful relationships based on openness and honesty. Likewise, my defense mechanism also prevents me from giving my full attention to the needs of others because I am so preoccupied with my own needs.

I'm learning open-heartedness, the ability to stay open to everything I experience so that I can fully honor others while living without barriers and controls. Open-heartedness doesn't mean I simply accept every control drama that others present to me. But it does mean that as I consider with patience any unproductive responses I may have accumulated, I am learning to communicate my thoughts and emotions more openly, and I am allowing others to do the same. I am learning to love and appreciate myself so that I am no longer as buffeted by the opinions of other people.

These days, criticism, at least constructive criticism, no longer feels like an attack on who I am but rather an attack on what I do and that's not nearly as frightening. Such criticism is an opportunity for me to see how others view my actions, allowing me the opportunity to decide for myself whether or not their input helps my journey. I can actually thank them for caring enough about me to want to help me grow. Even when their input seems like nothing more than a malicious attack, instead of seething with hurt or resentment I wonder what they are so afraid of that such anger or judgment could pour forth. I can choose to love them for where they are at on their journey knowing that if they knew how to love more they would.

More than anything, I am learning to be true to myself, and by doing this, I am able to be true to others as well.

Sometimes I still slip back into the old fear habits of self-protection and self-deception—pretending I'm okay with something when I'm not. But with patience I'm doing better all the time, and the difference in my self-respect is significant. Being honest and open-hearted makes me feel as if I'm really living life, not just existing or trying to stay safe. While learning to be patient and compassionate with myself, I find I am naturally able to be patient and compassionate with others as well.

Fellow travelers doing our very best to create new worlds from within, each one of us has our different challenges. Whatever these challenges may be, we all must negotiate uncharted territory. Our only certain guidance comes from the universal wisdom of Love, or God, coming to us as our own inner voice. We just need to be willing to listen and to trust.

Oh how we want someone to tell us exactly where and how to go! Teachers, guides, and books will give us some pointers in the right direction, but ultimately they are signposts helping us learn to follow our hearts and trust our deep spiritual wisdom. We can read the stories of other travelers and find at least some commonalities to give us courage to pursue our own quest. And we can support each other with open-hearted love and compassion.

Most importantly, because we are all waking up to the truth of who we already are as perfect, spiritual expressions of divine Love, with each step of this journey we will become more radiant, more vibrant and alive, more conscious of the beauty and creativity our lives are manifesting.

In Composing A Life, anthropologist, Mary Catherine Bateson provides a useful perspective on why, in the end, everyone will need to journey into this great unknown, letting go of predictability and certainty. She observes that we move through a landscape that is in constant flux. Children can't even know what careers will be available to them when they grow up.

"Goals too clearly defined can become blinkers . . . . Many of society's casualties are men and women who assumed they had chosen a path in life and found that it disappeared in the underbrush."

"In many ways," she says, "constancy is an illusion." And this is where the need for vision, courage, and patience arises. Right now we can let go of fear of the unknown, and embrace the joy and surprise inherent in evolving consciousness. This is a grand adventure and there is no doubt that we are getting to where we need to go.

Patience is a pre-requisite in this quest for spiritual growth but it doesn't necessitate boredom or even a slow pace. Ours is a grand quest with all its ups and downs, triumphs and trials. If we're brave each step of the way can be filled with adventure and new learning. While we have all decided to be more than armchair travelers and go beyond passively watching the journeys of others, most of us are probably relieved there is time to mature into these new experiences.

Spiritual journeys are tough for the faint-hearted. The faint-hearted might put a toe or two into the waters of change only to retreat back into their comfort zones, all the while hoping that someone will offer them an easier way. Perhaps someone will come along to provide the push and the shove they need.

While we might hope that divine Love, God, will provide this push and shove, that's not how God works. Remembering that divine Love, God, knows us only as she has created us—spiritual and perfect always—her push and shove is representative of how, when we reach a place in our spiritual journey where we are waking to the truth of who we are as Love's very evidence, we have no choice but to start to live this truth. We can no longer stand on the old shores. Holding onto the outmoded ways of anger and judgment, intolerance and fear, becomes painful. No matter how hard we cling to what we have always known, we simply can't live that way any more. Our old comfort zones are no longer comfortable. Living the old ways hurts.

We are literally forced out of these old ways when we see they no longer serve us. When we no longer want to suffer the consequences of living with tension and pain we have no choice but to discover new ways of being. We have no choice but to launch ourselves into the often-rough waters of change. As we muster up the courage to swim out, as we struggle to change our old perceptions, we gradually discover we can stay afloat; we can float free of the limits by which we thought we were trapped.

Patience is essential. So be kind to yourself if your progress seems too slow and you keep falling back into the old paradigms. After all, just turning on the TV can be enough to remind you of, and pull you back into, familiar habits of anger, revenge, deceit, competitiveness, judgment and intolerance. It can be extremely challenging to be different, to stand out from the masses still clinging to the old ways. At first it's really hard to remember there is another way of being, a way that embraces gentleness, tolerance, patience and kindness.

We need to watch out lest our new awareness takes on a holier than thou appearance, a sort of self-righteousness that becomes as exclusive and judgmental as the old ways from which we are breaking free. A vital part of this journey into living love is to get beyond the "us and them" mentality of separation, exclusivity and conceit. Intellectual knowing and higher education have never been prerequisites when it comes to living love.

As we continue our spiritual quest, if this different way of living is occasionally seen by others as ridiculous or boring—you know, the kindness, gentleness stuff—be patient with the critic. In time, they too may discover how exhilarating it is to live in open-hearted love, free from all the hurt and pain and fear that are part of the old ways. Remember that everyone is doing the very best they know how. When they know how to act differently they will act differently. We can be patient with them and with ourselves.

We can also be patient with ourselves when we find we are comparing our journey to the journeys of others, believing perhaps that others are making more rapid progress. It doesn't matter. We can never know what someone else is dealing with. We can't even know how long they've been on their journey. We must focus our efforts instead on living our journey the best we are able, always being true to ourselves. Comparison and judgment are part of the old paradigm.

If we're ever tempted to judge ourselves harshly for our lack of progress, just think about the sort of people with whom Jesus surrounded himself, his best friends even. His disciples certainly weren't the "perfect people" of this world. Getting close to a perfect person, a person trying to appear perfect, is impossible. We can't get too close because their barrier of perfection is designed to stop us. They don't want us to know they're really as imperfect as everyone else appears to be. Everyone has fears and doubts, frustrations and blocks. We all have good days and bad days.

I know this because I used to try very hard to be perfect. I ended up with what appeared to be, in other people's eyes, the perfect family life, the perfect home and the perfect career. It wasn't until just a few years ago that I started to realize I wasn't really *living*. I didn't actually know who I was or what I wanted. I had spent most of my adult life trying to be who I thought others wanted me to be. I hardly ever formed my own opinions because my opinions were mirrored through what other people thought. Therefore being on my own was scary because I didn't know how to think for myself. My life looked perfect, and on a superficial level at least it was happy. It's possible to be happy pleasing everyone and being very good. It's not a lasting, deep down joy though, and I used to feel very guilty as if I *should* feel happier than I did. I even felt I was selfish if I wasn't grateful for my wonderful life! I thought, "Other people would be grateful in my situation."

And so the endless cycle of self-criticism and condemnation for never quite measuring up to what I thought I *should* be achieving continued. Incidentally, we need to watch out for unwarranted should's and ought-to's in our vocabulary. They can indicate that we're not thinking or speaking for ourselves. We're probably voicing tribal, cultural, social, or family expectations that, if we're honest, may not resonate with our own highest sense of truth.

I know this problem of endless self-criticism that we're not measuring up to what we *should* be achieving is familiar territory for many of you reading this book. Take heart. Even if you don't think you've begun to find a way out, you have—or you wouldn't be reading this. If I was able to find a way out, you can too—if you're patient with yourself.

Even from the first weeks of determining to live my life differently, I wouldn't go back for anything. My life might not look as perfect as it used to but the difference is enormous. I am living fully, loving fully, and I have an increasingly ingrained sense of joy and freedom that is exquisite—even when I'm scared, lost and kicking myself in the shins because I've forgotten that this is a lifetime journey and I need to be patient.

As I said earlier in the chapter, it may take years, or lifetimes even, to reach a consistent level of spiritual knowing where a physical or bodily state of being no longer serves us and we simply move into a purely spiritual state of being. Before we reach any sort of consistency we may flip flop between moments of spiritual clarity and lengthy periods of living the old dreams.

There's no point in getting down about it. What matters is that we're gently and patiently expanding the moments of clarity. We can't force this process. We will notice over time that we gradually trust more and gain greater peace. Increasingly, we simply know what our truth is and begin to live it, often quite unconsciously. We begin to notice we are expecting to heal discordant situations. We expect to be guided in taking whatever steps lead to our highest good. We expect to be healthy and active. And when we're not, we expect to hear whatever insights we need to break the dream of discord. And, even then, when we find ourselves still lost in the dream, we are patient with ourselves, glad that, despite all of this confusion, we are still learning, growing and throwing off the chains that bind us.

As we come closer to a consistent understanding that spiritual perfection is our true identity we also learn that everything in our lives unfolds in its perfect timing. There is a sense of peace that comes with this knowing. And as our understanding of spiritual reality moves to each new level of awareness, the events of our day-to-day human living conform to this increasing spiritual consciousness of harmony. Patience is simply letting this unfolding continue in its perfect timing, without resistance or struggle, until at last we feel we really are living love and are uncovering that longed for joy, freedom and peace.

Affirmation on loving your precious God Self

I am able to be so comfortable with the beautiful and whole person I am—not just with my talents and what I do, but who I AM as this unique, amazing being created by Love to express herself. It is impossible for me to be anything less than Love's perfect creation, impossible to disappoint my Creator, impossible to be anything but LOVE. I am so comfortable with this precious Love-created Self that what other people think about me doesn't matter. They are on their journeys and I am on mine.

I strive to reach my dreams and my highest knowing, aware that my sense of worth and acceptance is not dependent on anything outside my own consciousness.

And when I fall short of my expectations this is okay too because I am able to be patient, forgiving, gentle and compassionate with myself just as I would be with someone I love dearly. The love I pour out to another person is the same love that I pour out to my own beloved Self.

As I remember this is who I am now and always have been, I effortlessly relax into my day-to-day experiences with joy, humor and playfulness. I dance through each day, not only with a sense of fun and lightness but also with an overflowing awareness of deep fulfillment, sometimes even tear-filled amazement and humility at the beauty of my present life. I have boundless ability to focus on what brings me true worth and delight. With an open heart I embrace abundant, everlasting life and love. With true joy and ease, I bring to the world my great and unique gifts.

PART THREE

UNDERSTANDING OUR TRUE

IDENTITY AND PURPOSE

AS LOVE'S EXPRESSION

CHAPTER 11

DROPPING THE MASKS

Insist on yourself; never imitate
Ralph Waldo Emerson

A WOMAN, ANGELA, CAME TO SEE ME NOT LONG AFTER I STARTED my healing practice. She was a successful businesswoman, a pillar of her church, a wonderful entertainer, always so gracious, always beautifully dressed, always doing good deeds. Although I'd known her for years, somehow I'd always found her rather remote and hard to get close to. As she sat down in my office, she explained she'd had a lot of pain in one leg for years and had not found a cure. She'd always relied on spiritual healing for her health care and wanted to continue to do so, but she could not understand why she had not been healed.

As she was talking it struck me that she was wearing a mask. Behind this image of a perfect, happy woman her eyes showed something quite different. There was a deep sadness visible. I gently asked her, "why are you so sad?" She recoiled almost as if I'd hit her and was silent, struggling to know what to say. I remained quiet, affirming her actual identity as Love's expression, feeling clearly that her real beauty and goodness are spiritual, and that she could find joy in this awareness. I was imbued with a vivid sensation of God's ever-present tenderness guiding this child.

Shortly she sank back onto the couch and started to cry quietly and uncontrollably. I moved to sit beside her and put my arm around her, continuing to affirm her spiritual identity. After a short while she became still. She began to apologize, telling me she'd never allowed herself to cry before and saw it as a sign of weakness. I suggested that, on the contrary, tears could be seen as a sign of strength and courage, a willingness to express her deepest feelings and emotions and open her heart and soul to being who she truly was. With this emotional honesty she would open floodgates of profound inner joy and freedom.

She pondered this radically different perspective thoughtfully, and as I watched, her barriers and rigidity started to fall away. I knew this was the start of the healing of the pain as well. More often than not, pain and other physical problems are simply indicators of painful, tense or blocked thinking. Such obstructed thinking can show up as obstructed bodily functions. We need to remember a problem never originates in body but in thought. When we harmonize thought we harmonize body. Our ultimate aim is not to heal matter, but to correct the assumption that matter is real in the first place.

Since working with Angela I have enjoyed seeing the warmth, joy and spontaneity that increasingly radiates from her. She doesn't need my help to do this. Once we obtain even a small glimpse of our true selfhood, nothing can stop our desire to discover more of this emerging identity. It is as though we come home to who we are and our arrival brings great peace, joy and freedom. Angela tells me she feels a tangible sense of relief and lightness that comes from no longer needing to keep a barrier or mask in place. She has discovered that the people who matter in her life love her as she is —even when she's not doing everything right. "Why was it so hard before?" she wonders.

Being someone we're not is difficult. Second-guessing how we think we're supposed to be at every moment is stressful. After years of unconsciously masking her true self, and suffering the consequences, Angela is now increasingly open and aware of her spiritual identity, of who she really is and what she is here to do. Living her truth in this way is restful—energizing even.

As we continue to awaken to our spiritual identity our masks naturally and effortlessly fall away. But such awakening requires patience because we are so conditioned by our culture to act a certain way, talk a certain way, think a certain way, and in western culture at least, be successful, beautiful, handsome, and so on. Because most of us cannot live up to these expectations, we create masks for ourselves in an effort to approximate these social or, as Carolyn Myss puts it, tribal expectations as best as we can.

Because we're so conditioned to pretend to be who our masks claim we are we don't even notice what we've done. These masks have often been in place since childhood, so of course we've grown used to them and fail to notice their presence. And yet we wonder why we're not as content as we could be. We feel a sort of underlying guilt because either consciously or unconsciously we know we're living a lie. If only I could be perfect like other people I know. I *should* be perfect—other people are. Why can't I be this way? And so the unconscious deception and hurt continues.

Little children don't live this lie. They get tired and cranky, they scream with delight, they scream with frustration, they dance and sing in public places. At any moment they simply *are* what their emotions tell them they are. And to begin with this is okay. But then the socializing starts and adults condition children to how they are supposed to be.

At a very elegant restaurant one night, I watched a little boy of about two or three skip and sing his way towards the exit, no doubt relieved to be able to escape the ordeal of sitting quietly for an hour or so. Lost in his own world of joy, he was accosted by his mother who, in a very audible self-conscious whisper, scolded him for being naughty and disturbing people. His little bubble burst, his shoulders dropped, and his dear little face lost its sparkle. Dragging his feet, he left the restaurant in the firm hand of his life instructor. I felt so sad. That tiny light of spontaneous joy was gone just as quickly as it had illuminated the whole room with its promise. I wondered how long it would take before this little guy tuned back into his own emotions and came back to his true self.

Because our children continue to be born into a world that has forgotten that all our needs are already met in the oneness of Love, they also learn early to fear not having enough. They learn to hold onto their toys and demand attention in whatever ways they can. Because of this consciousness of limitation, before long they need to be socialized to live in harmony with others. The challenge then becomes how to allow for and celebrate uniqueness and individuality, so that children are not tempted to don masks simply to conform to societal expectations that simply do not matter.

There is such a temptation to opt for sameness. We opt for a mask of conformity, approval and acceptance by our tribe, even when we inwardly know that we are selling our souls to do so. The tribe of contemporary western civilization places a high value on individual competition and success, fame and fortune. Once we realize that living love, living in harmony with others and valuing diversity, is more important to us than the social approval of the tribe, living this conformity becomes increasingly impossible. We must find a balance that reflects our notion of truth. Sameness just won't do any more.

There's a wonderful little book by Michael Yaconelli called *messy spirituality* that speaks to this.

> Sameness is a disease with disastrous consequences—differences are ignored, uniqueness is not listened to, our gifts are cancelled out. Life, passion, and joy are snuffed out. Sameness . . . flattens the human race, franchises us, attempts to make us all homogenous . . .. In a sea of sameness, no one has an identity.

The little boy in the restaurant surely had his joy snuffed out—at least for the moment.

We each have magnificent and unique gifts we bring to this life. If anything is our *duty*, surely it is to share this abundance with openheartedness, to be who we came to be.

As we grow in awareness of who we actually are, we realize that by living behind the masks of sameness and acceptability we do not live the truth of who we are. As we become aware of these masks and are willing at last to drop them and march to our own beat, we start to explore the wondrous territory of what we came here to do—we witness our purpose and vision, that which truly makes our hearts sing and our eyes light up.

That we have been masking our true identities by living behind masks of acceptability is a complete mystery for many of us who have lived much of our lives following the "sameness" code. I was certainly not aware I did this. My search to discover my transcendent spiritual identity and purpose accelerated only in the last few years. Prior to a period of tremendous personal upheaval, I lived behind a mask much of the time. I did a superb job of living the life of the woman I was expected to be. Consequently, I now realize how I missed out on so many potentially incredible experiences that would have helped me discover my true selfhood. Still, everything has its perfect timing, and at that point in my life I was doing exactly what I needed to do in order to move forward into a greater awareness of my purpose and identity.

In what I now call my "old life," success was always vitally important to me. I felt I would not be loved or accepted if I wasn't good at everything I did. By avoiding anything I might not be good at, I was successful at almost everything I did. By nature I have always been a happy and optimistic person, and to almost everyone else it seemed as if I had a perfect life. I appeared to have everything anyone could possibly want—a perfect home life, family and career.

Why then, in those last few years, had I become increasingly discontented? And why did I feel so guilty for being unhappy when, after all, look at everything I had? "Surely," I thought, "I must be very self-centered to be so ungrateful. Anyone else in my shoes would be quite blissful. What is wrong with me?" And so it went on, day after day, year after year. My innate joy was beginning to wither.

I still continued to do effective healing and spiritual mentoring work for others. I had grown up relying on metaphysical healing for all health care needs and my confidence in this did not change. Still, I was perplexed as to why, despite this confidence, my happiness increasingly eluded me.

Gradually I started to see that while I felt I knew who I was as a spiritual expression of divine Love, my knowing wasn't heart-centered. I was not living *my* truth or *my* life. I was doing what was necessary to meet others' expectations of who I should be and what I should do. I was certainly a valuable and successful tribe member, but if only I could listen to my own heart and have the courage to march to my own beat, I knew I could do so much more. I recognized that in order to do this, I first needed to find myself. But how would I cope with the disapproval, the condemnation and the accusations of selfishness during this time of what seemed like a mid-life crisis? How could I possibly cope with my fears of rejection and not being loved?

While stepping out of the old way of doing things seemed overwhelming, staying with the old ways was not possible either. I felt like a fraud. I became more and more uncomfortable and unhappy, feeling I was living in a world that was no longer mine. Eventually I had no choice and felt forcibly propelled away from everything I had known.

I had to emerge into my true identity by discovering and living my true purpose. I was working with clients and helping them do this. I knew it was now my time to live what I taught. I felt like Alice in Wonderland falling down the rabbit hole. I had no handholds to grab onto, nothing to stop me from falling into a void. I could see nothing ahead of me, nor could I return to where I had been. My old comfort zone no longer served me. I had to let go of everything I had been holding onto as security. To stay put would be to annihilate my soul.

I stepped away from my old life and as frightening as this was, at last I felt as if I was really living. I felt as if the whole Universe had stepped in to support me. The most incredible open-hearted, loving and self-aware people I had ever met started turning up in my life to guide and encourage me, and although I hadn't known any of them very long, I felt as if each one was a lifelong friend. So many gifted, and have continued to gift me unique insights about who I am and where I am going. Very early on in my journey, for instance, a very special new friend, Emmanuel, sent me a copy of Ralph Waldo Emerson's "Essay on Self-reliance." A number of passages, such as the following, resonated deeply:

Whoso would be a man, must be a non conformist . . .. What I must do is all that concerns me, not what people think . . .. To be great is to be misunderstood . . .. Insist on yourself; never imitate.... That which each can do best, none but his Maker can teach him.

With such inspiration and love to guide me, an exhilarating journey began, full of incredible synchronistic events. Time is quite irrelevant in the journey to spiritual enlightenment. In one sense, I lost most of the material props I believed were necessary for happiness, and yet I felt richer and more stable than I ever had previously. Now I am no longer frightened of losing home or income or the approval of others—I've already lost all these things, only to feel freer than ever. I'm no longer trapped by unfounded fears in a life and culture that I can no longer serve.

Throughout this period of re-designing my life, I never once doubted the spiritual principles I hold to. I never drifted from my desire to help others nor did my ability to effectively heal others become compromised. In fact, more and more people have continued to come to me for help with re-designing *their* lives. I have shared my own struggles to find a new footing as openly and as honestly as possible. My authentic life, my "realness" seems to have given others the courage to be true to themselves. Such "realness" is an essential element in finding our spiritual identity and dropping our masks. Instead of merely imparting the "head stuff" of theory and so-called knowledge, I can now also speak from my heart and from my experience.

Out of this growing self awareness I have come to see clearly the pitfalls of putting on masks of perfection to try to emulate how we think we're supposed to be. Not only can living a lie hurt others, it can also cause us considerable stress and discomfort. I used to get frequent headaches until one day my friend, Mary Hunt, suggested that perhaps I only got headaches when I wasn't telling my truth. I became more careful about speaking only what was true to me, or, as Miguel Ruiz terms it in *The Four Agreements,* being impeccable with my word. The headaches almost completely disappeared.

In a culture that rewards fame and fortune, beauty and brains, feeling like a failure is easy and all too common. In reality, few people ever meet the requirements of societal success. Life becomes a struggle to find satisfaction or fulfillment. Young girls grow up wanting to look like fashion models, oblivious to the fact that many fashion models live in silent hidden misery to keep up appearances. It is sad that many will never be able to bear children because they have starved themselves for so long.

So many people work ludicrous hours to bring in enough money to provide all the toys that success is supposed to bring. In the process, the rewarding pleasures of family life, the development of solid relationships, and the time for inspiration and spiritual renewal are very often completely denied. We chase false gods. We hide our pain behind masks of acceptability and society's image of success.

I have found this obsession with perfection pervades the church I grew up in—and actually threatens its survival. Because the teachings of Christian Science distinguish between our true spiritual selfhood and our present perception of a limited physical selfhood, we can be tempted to believe that if we're not demonstrating rapid attainment of our spiritual growth through physical and emotional perfection, we are not good church members. For many people, this brings guilt and a harsh fear of failure, heaviness, and stress. They deal with it, mostly unconsciously, by donning their masks of acceptability and success, maintaining a certain emotional distance from others, and refusing to talk about their struggles. They only share their triumphs. I know from my own experience and from the experiences of clients like Angela: perfect clothes and smiles often hide great unhappiness and frustration.

Yes, when we're praying to see the spiritual reality behind a discordant condition, telling others that we have a problem is counterproductive *if* our friends and neighbors are only going to make it more of a reality by adding their own doubts and fears. On the other hand, if, with compassion and care, they can help ease our fears and remind us of how we are really perfect, spiritual expressions of divine Love, then sharing our challenges can enable us to progress more quickly.

Genuine sharing demonstrates that we are willing to live in com-

munity, loving and supporting each other without criticism and condemnation. We get beyond the dualistic judgments of good and bad,
right and wrong, and simply accept that we're all doing the very best
we know how at any given moment. When we can do better, we will.
In the meantime we carry each other when we need help. There is
release and comfort in such knowing and caring.

When we parade the mask of our perfect image, we often alien-
ate others, albeit unintentionally. Our image just doesn't feel authentic. Anyone in tune with their feelings recognizes the facade. This sham
is one reason why so many young people leave organized religion in
their teens or early twenties, and why so few of today's spiritual seekers who realize the importance of feelings and find religious teachings valuable, avoid organized religion.

I've had many clients who withdrew from church because they
simply felt guilty and inadequate. They felt they just weren't good
enough. It never occurred to them that the "perfect people" are probably not doing any better than they are. If these perfect people were
honest with themselves, most would find they are actually desperate
for a comforting hug and unconditional acceptance. They yearn to
share their doubts and fears, but they just can't risk removing their
masks and exposing themselves for fear of rejection. No wonder some
churches and their members exhibit little emotion and a sense of re-
moteness. Too much head stuff and not enough heart.

But it doesn't need to be this way. Mary Baker Eddy says that
the heart and soul of Christian Science is love. While she certainly
knew the power of love, as explained in her book, *Science and Health*,
a rigidity of interpretation over the ensuing century has replaced much
of the original inspiration and sense of joy that early followers experienced. As a friend of mine said, "All this love and no nurturing.
Wow!"

Of course it is not just the Christian Science churches that suffer from these problems of cold formality and judgment. As society
sheds off many of its more formal Victorian behaviors, all churches,
in order to survive, must do likewise. Spiritual seeking today is pri-
marily about the heart and soul rather than the intellectual theory that
has dominated the Christian church for so long. Ultimately, intellec-

tual theory and loving practice must go hand in hand, but for now spiritual seekers are redressing the balance by seeking out love and caring, community and non-judgment wherever it may be found.

Our churches can be places of unconditional acceptance and nurturing, providing a safe haven for those of us struggling just to meet our own expectations, let alone anyone else's expectations. Fortunately, many churches are becoming increasingly aware of this need and are responding with love.

We must become emotionally honest with ourselves and with each other. We must nurture and care for ourselves and others. I have yet to meet a perfect person who is still on this plane of existence. We are all learning what we need for our journey and each one of us is right where we need to be at any given moment. As we drop our masks and are true to ourselves and others, this world will become a very different place—a place of compassion and gentle loving kindness. It must happen—it is just a question of when.

Perfect timing for each of the events of our lives exists. There was the right time for Angela to begin her journey to self-awareness. There was the right time for me to begin mine. And there is the right time for you. Love will never abandon us nor leave us to cope alone. When we step over the precipice to fly free of the old ways, to discover how to live our true identity and purpose, the whole universe, the universal energy of Love, comes to our aid, keeping us safe and supported until we find our new footing.

A few years after the start of this journey, I have a much firmer grasp on who I am and what I came here to do. I have a much stronger understanding of my spiritual identity as Love's reflection. I love what I do. I know I could not have reached this place without first being willing to drop the masks that had served me for the first half of my life.

How did I first become aware of the mask of "acceptability" I was wearing? By becoming increasingly discontented with my life even though I had no idea why I felt the way I did. Several years passed before I reached a point where I could understand that I was being forced to discover who was behind the mask. I was compelled to start revealing my true identity and live my life purpose.

Thankfully, there are people who grow up in very accepting environments where there is never a need to don these masks of tribal acceptance. Right from babyhood their feelings are validated, not evaluated. They are not told they should or should not be feeling what they are feeling. They are taught that all feelings are valid regardless of whether they are labeled "good" feelings or "bad" feelings. These children are honored simply for who they are. Parents who have struggled to develop a greater self-awareness themselves are now allowing their children the space and freedom to also grow into greater self-awareness.

This is no mere coincidence but the result of a rapidly growing spiritual awakening happening on the planet—sometimes called the New Age that came into its fullness at the beginning of this millennium.

Most cultures accept that little children live in fantasy worlds where their imaginations enable tremendous vision and creativity. By a certain age, however, children are told that believing in fairies and make-believe friends is childish. Most children heed the reprimand for fear of being thought immature and they soon forget they ever really saw or believed these things.

I remember two summers ago taking a long hike with a young friend up a mountain beside a sun-dappled stream. In this magical setting I asked her if she could see any fairies or other little people. She stopped and stared hard at me, trying to ascertain if I was teasing her. Deciding I was not, she quickly scanned our surroundings to see if anyone else was in earshot, and then whispered that I must promise not to tell anyone or they would think she was a baby, but yes, sometimes she still could see things she wasn't supposed to. She could see her make-believe friend and she could sometimes still see fairies—but not often now because it was hard to see them when people kept telling her they weren't real. When I told her I wished I could still see what she saw, she gave my hand a quick squeeze and reassured me that they could still see me.

The increasing number of children who are allowed to trust their feelings and inner knowing are often called mystic, indigo or psychic children. These children have an acute awareness of not only who they are and of what they are here to do, but also of spiritual truth and the vital importance of living love.

While I have worked in recent years with many young people whom I consider to be indigo children, most of these have been college age men and women. I have also met a number of older people who have an acute awareness of their identity and purpose—no doubt the "advance guard" of the New Age that heralds the rapidly growing need to live in harmony and oneness on the planet. While the emergence of so many mystic or indigo children confirms this phenomenon, we are all involved in this trend. As we drop our masks, all of us are able to discover how to live with passion and delight, allowing our feelings and emotions to mean something. Developing our own inner knowing and self-awareness, we walk the pathway to knowing clearly our true purpose in this life.

Even though developing an awareness of the masks we use enables us to begin dropping them, it is imperative that we relinquish the thought patterns that created these masks in the first place. This process, however, can only be accomplished on our own. Searching for someone to tell us what to do will only aid us to a limited extent. No two journeys are alike. There are wonderful guides and amazing books full of the wisdom and stories of others' personal experiences, but in the end these resources simply provide encouragement for what we must largely accomplish on our own. When we value our unique niche in creation we will welcome the adventure that comes with discovering for ourselves the fullness of our radiant being.

One of the multitude of amazing books that have helped me on my journey to self-awareness is Margaret Wheatley's *Leadership and the New Science: Discovering Order in a Chaotic World*. She explains a concept I found vital in understanding the transformation that was happening to me. The concept, put simply, is that harmony always emerges from apparent chaos. This chaos, which frees us from our past ways of doing things, is necessary to create a new order. The old ways no longer make sense to us. I can certainly relate to this observation! Setting out on a spiritual journey is no armchair ride and sometimes it can feel very lonely. As Wheatley observes, exploration used to be easier. We could pay someone else to do our exploring for us and have them bring home the knowledge and treasures we sought.

> We still want to work this way; we still look to take what others
> have discovered and adopt it as our own. But we have all learned
> from experience that solutions don't transfer . . .. We are required
> to go down to the dock and begin our individual journeys.

She goes on to say that we need to share what we find so others can learn what is possible as they search for their own treasure.

There are no magic formulas. Each of us must find our own path to truth and we do this, not by internalizing endless theories or by reading endless books or attending endless workshops, but by paying attention to our *feelings*, and listening to what resonates deep within our own heart. There is simply no other way.

Gradually as we turn away from our preoccupation with logic and intellect, we find there is only love to guide us, and it dawns on us that love is all we could ever want or need. At last we listen to what in our inner depths calls to us and says, "follow your heart." We pay attention to the feelings that propel us with delight down a certain path even when there is no end in sight, no visible, safe outcome. We notice what brings us unfathomable peace when there seems no logical reason for it.

Likewise, we pay attention to what causes us emotional pain. Pushing away or ignoring feelings of tension, grief, anger, sadness and frustration deprives us of important indicators that tell us the condition of our thought. Emotional pain may also identify the masks we are wearing when we are not living or speaking our truth. So often this tension or frustration seeks to blame other people or circumstances for our pain when the cause is always within our own hearts. In forgetting, even momentarily, that Love provides our every need, our hearts may again become full of fear and, for an instant, at least, we lose sight of our spiritual identity and purpose. Going down this painful path is okay. Even when it feels as though we are taking backward steps, we are actually still moving forward steadily and dropping our masks.

We need to keep asking the questions that help us identify and drop our masks. Why am I resisting this particular circumstance? Why do I feel insecure? What is behind my feeling of possessiveness?

Thinking about the answers to such *feeling* questions and digging deeper beneath the layers of old conditioning, sensible solutions, the perceived influence of others, and caution, begins to provide us with our own answers in the discovery and relinquishment of our masks. We start to come home to our spiritual identity and purpose. With persistence and reflection we begin at last to discern our magnificence.

Each step in dropping our masks propels us forward on this journey to self-awareness. The benefits of this inner growth include the resulting bliss that manifests as we learn more about our spiritual identity as pure expressions of divine Love. The closer we are to living love and living in harmony with ourselves and others in this human experience, the closer we are to mirroring the spiritual truth of who we really are. When we remember what is already true—our present perfection—no masks, limits or fears can bind us or hinder our growth. We experience pure joy, freedom and peace.

Talking with God

True: Dear Father-Mother, you say you will not leave me, but why can't I get beyond the grief and the pain of so much hurt? Why can't I feel the joy, peace and love that must be mine as your child? Why is my life so unhappy right now when all around me there is beauty, joy and harmony? Why can't I remember who I am as your spiritual child?

God: Because you are mesmerized by hurt and sadness, by the belief that you are a mortal in a material body instead of knowing that you are my child, a beloved, perfect spiritual being. You have forgotten for the moment that you are always surrounded by angel thoughts guiding you gently and reminding you who you are. You possess only the mind of absolute perfection, wisdom and understanding. Nothing in your being is limited, restricted or subject to chance and change. You are able to hear the Christ Truth pouring into your consciousness telling you what you need to know as you awaken from this dream. This Christ consciousness obliterates all unhappy thinking and replaces it with the peace, joy and power of perfect harmony. There is no separation between us. I am divine Love and you are Love's pure expression.

You cannot know anything but perfect good. This is the truth of being and it has behind it all the power of divine perfection. Love is the source of all your satisfaction, safety, joy, peace of mind, fulfillment, direction and harmony. You have all the completeness of infinite perfection right now and forever. Nothing can change this.

Just trust, dear One. I will never abandon you. I cannot. There is no separation. Everything I AM, you are. Everything I AM is yours because we are One.

CHAPTER 12

I AM NOT WHAT I DO

We do not see things as they are, we see things as we are.

The Talmud

A S I KEEP REITERATING, IDENTITY AND PURPOSE ARE FULLY IN-
tertwined and it is impossible to understand one without
the other. When we understand our true identity then our purpose,
what we are here to do, becomes clear to us. Likewise, when we acquire a clear sense of what we are here to do, we also acquire a much
clearer vision of who we truly are. Despite the intertwining of identity and purpose, it is important to see that identity and purpose are
not the same.

One of the difficulties we face when we question our purpose
or life direction is that we confuse what we do with who we are. We
think other people identify us by our roles and occupations.

I have had to work hard at being able to say and understand,

I am not what I do.

I used to think that my spiritual identity was somehow tied up
with the roles I played—wife, mother, business woman, spiritual
healer, friend, colleague, and so on. I believed that people identified
me only by these roles. It is true many people probably do, but as I
consciously express increasing emotional honesty people are able to
discover who I really am. I am no longer seen only by what I do.

The problem with identifying ourselves by what we do is that success becomes critical to our self-image. When we mess up, make mistakes and don't perform according to our expectations, our feeling of failure reflects directly back on our sense of who we are. We identify ourselves as failures or inadequate when, in fact, all that has happened is that we have failed or done inadequately at something we needed to do. When we can separate the two we do not condemn ourselves. Our self worth remains intact and we continue to recognize the amazing and magnificent being we are, even when this amazing and magnificent being does not accomplish what we originally intended.

As we are able to separate who we are from what we do, and as we continue to discover more about our spiritual identity, our inherent purpose inevitably becomes clearer to us. Less and less we confuse who we are with what we do. Our identity becomes clearer all the time and is less dependent on the roles we perform or the achievements or failures of our "doing." Despite this self-awareness, discovering what we love to do can still take plenty of persistence.

There's a lovely letter to a young writer by Rainer Maria Rilke in *Letters to a Young Poet*. The message of the letter epitomizes the passion that comes from living our purpose and vision. To help discover what your purpose may be, you can substitute the word "write" in the following with your own word or phrase about what you love to do most in your life. Try reading this passage and leaving a pause or substituting different words for "write."

> There is only one way: Go within. Search for the cause, find the impetus that bids you to write. Put it to this test: Does it stretch out its roots in the deepest place of your heart? Can you vow that you would die if you were forbidden to write? Above all, in the most silent hour of your night, ask yourself this: MUST I write? Dig deep into yourself for a true answer. And if it should ring its assent, if you can confidently meet this serious question with a simple, "I must," then build your life upon it. It has become your necessity. Your life, in even the most mundane and least significant hour, must become a sign, a testimony to this urge.

I love to go through this exercise with clients and friends. You may quickly find what it is that propels you out of bed in the morning, without which you would just feel like dying if you were forbidden to do. When I read this letter inserting "discovering truth," I feel a marvelous upwelling of joy and freedom within me—a lightness even. My friend, Max, inserts the word "reconcile" with the same results.

Often when I ask clients what they love to do most, they quickly tell me what they don't enjoy doing. According to my friends, Jim and June Spencer, founders and directors of the Let Go and Live Institute, most people have no idea at all what they want to do with their lives or even what they love to do. They are focused on what they don't want to do and what they don't have. In other words, their consciousness is filled with lack and discontent. A consciousness of lack produces experiences that reflect this lack. Experience mirrors thought. These people experience the very things they are running from.

Ultimately, discovering what we love to do rather than holding onto what we despise the most, is the most critical step in our quest for identity and purpose. I often ask clients to take a large sheet of paper and write all over it the things they love to do and the things that fill them with delight. Because they are fixated on what they don't like, sometimes it takes a long time for them to get started. They can find it quite upsetting to realize they can't think of a thing to put down.

I was introduced to this exercise a few years ago when I met a new and utterly delightful friend, Mary Hunt, who runs a business consultancy in Auckland, New Zealand. One part of her work includes helping clients discover their purpose—what they love, or would love, to do most. At the time she introduced me to this exercise, I was at a very difficult early stage of my spiritual journey. Mary really had her work cut out getting me over this hump of despair at not knowing what I loved to do. I sat there with my blank piece of paper for what seemed like hours. Eventually I wrote "watching clouds." I love gazing at clouds. Then I wrote "listening to music." Music, many styles of music, has always filled me with ecstasy.

As I worked on my sheet of paper over weeks, it felt as if each time I wrote something the mist, the murkiness, became less dense. Gradually I could get past clouds and music to pinpointing the things I loved to do such as my constant search for truth and my healing and teaching work. It's not that I hadn't loved to do them—it was just that I took them for granted and hadn't actually realized how passionate I was about them. I recognized how much I loved sharing what I was discovering and watching others light up just as I was.

I realized how I had been so focused on what I didn't love in my life rather than on what I did, that my limited focus had become a habit, an attitude of despondency and lack. As I identified how much I loved my healing and guidance work, I found a growing, even exciting urge to focus on it rather than on the things I was running from. My thought became filled with abundance and this abundance began to manifest in my day-to-day life. No wonder I felt I was living at last!

Try doing this exercise. Write a love list and don't be put off if it takes a while to get started. It will help you start to discover who you really are, what you love to do, and how you love to be. This initial discovery is an enormous step forward in dropping the masks that would hinder you on your path towards greater self-awareness, healing and joy.

Read Rilke's poem again, this time not so much for a word to clue you into your passionate purpose, but simply to get a sense of the excitement behind this journey of discovering your true identity. What is the "impetus that bids you" step out from the tribe, drop your masks, and find the joy, freedom and peace that come with discovering who you truly are and what you are here to do? Can you vow that you would die if you were forbidden to start to sing and dance in the joy of this quest? MUST I . . . set forth on this journey even though I have no idea where it is going? MUST I build my life upon this? "Your life, in even the most mundane and least significant hour, must become a sign, a testimony to this urge."

Even just writing this, I get the urge to yell "yes!!!!" at the top of my voice. You see, my journey reflects my oftentimes exuberant nature. For others, their journeys may be all about deep peace and introspection. Trust your own feelings and you have your best guide with you. I promise you that the answers to everything you need to know to make this journey are right within your own heart. My experiences will be different from yours but I hope they may give you pointers along your way that inspire you to seek your true identity and purpose, to discover what it is you love to do. Then your work becomes your play.

In a book called *Making a Life, Making a Living,* Mark Albion discusses a study of business school graduates that illustrates the effect of making a career out of what we love to do. Starting in 1960 fifteen hundred graduates had their careers tracked over a twenty-year period. From the outset of the study, students were grouped into two categories. Category A included graduates who chose to get financial security before doing what they really loved to do. Category B included those who chose to pursue what they really wanted to do from the outset, sure that success would follow. Of the fifteen hundred graduates, 83% fell into Category A and only 17% in Category B. After twenty years there were 101 millionaires. One was in Category A— the security first category—and 100 were in Category B—do what you love from the outset.

Doing what we love to do may seem like play but it can also be profitable when we get our priorities straight.

Back in 1999 one of my sons, Shaun, completed his masters degree in marine biology. The question then arose, what was he going to pursue as a career? In New Zealand at the time there were far more marine science graduates than there were jobs. Nevertheless, he was offered a job working with fisheries—not exciting, but at least it was reasonably well paid. Shaun was standing firmly on the same ground as the business students in Category A— he was hoping to obtain security first. The only problem was that no matter how Shaun justified this decision, he could not feel comfortable with it. My brother, Kit, and his wife, Ruth, visited around this time, and upon hearing the dilemma, Ruth asked, "But what are you passionate about doing?" Up until this time Shaun had been completely immersed in his studies and in his outdoor interests like surfing, scuba diving, climbing and just about any other extreme sport available in the country. As he fumbled around trying to think what he was passionate about doing, other than sport, I noticed his eyes start to light up and a growing excitement in his voice.

What he loved to do most, he saw, was to teach. He'd taught a kayaking course over the previous summer for inner city kids who'd never done anything like it before. He had loved every moment of teaching this course, watching each child discover their potential and purpose.

The change in his attitude was immediate. He went from a sort of passive acceptance of his situation to eager anticipation and determination to follow his dream.

However, despite vigorous efforts to find such work, there were absolutely no openings. The fisheries job was still the only secure option. So we both prayed to know that because he clearly understood his spiritual identity as an expression of the universal energy of Love, it was inevitable that he would be able to fulfill his life purpose. Financial security was not the priority, even though it would certainly come when needed.

Shortly after, during a trip to the United States, I heard that a summer camp in Maine, where some young friends of mine were working, needed a climbing instructor urgently. Camp was about to start. I knew how Shaun would love this work and I suggested he might like to check out this job possibility. He called and was immediately offered the position—on a voluntary basis because he wouldn't be able to get a work permit—if he could get there within two days. As his current fisheries contract had just finished and trusting his financial needs would somehow be met, he flew out a few hours later and spent an incredible summer fulfilling his dream of helping young people.

He returned to New Zealand in September, as required by the immigration services, and was given another six-month fisheries contract. While this work certainly didn't fulfill his new vision and purpose, he continued to trust that in its perfect timing, the right career path would appear. During this time he was offered a much more lucrative and interesting position by a different company, but as he was still under contract, he felt it would be unethical to take the better job. As disappointed as he felt, he prayed to know he could not suffer from doing what seemed the highest right.

Just as his contract was about to end, he received a call from another summer camp in the United States asking whether, if they could get him a work visa, he would be willing to come and work for them fulltime for eighteen months. Again he would be teaching the extreme sports he loved most. Within a month he was in Colorado. It seemed like a dream come true and it was. No dreams are ever too good to be true. Fulfilling our dreams depends upon our expectations.

Currently Shaun enjoys teaching biology at a Midwestern college. As it turned out he had the courage and vision to become a Category B graduate—do what he loved to do from the outset, trusting that success would follow.

When we follow our life direction our path is deeply fulfilling.

The mystic philosopher, Meister Eckhart, once said that when he returns to the godhead from which he came he will not be judged on his work so much as on his being. "Think more about who you are and less about what you do," he counsels, "for if you are just your ways will be just."

This reference comes from a book I have found fascinating in understanding more about what we are here to do—Matthew Fox's *The Reinvention of Work*.

Fox warns against accepting work that is too small for us, that does not engender deep passion in us. Such work, he says, is "drudgery without meaning" that produces nothing worthwhile.

"When our work is small it can never satisfy souls that yearn for the vast vortexes of the divine, that derive new life from the wild works of life, new truth from the sacred wilderness of our experiences."

I love this idea of expansive, soul-stretching work as adventure. He goes on to say that if there is no passion in our work, we may have a job but we have not yet found our work. Joy is an essential part of this work. Fox continues:

"Our work deserves to go beyond the tame and out into the wilderness. This is another way of saying that we must include the Spirit in our work. Spirit does not like safe and cozy harbors."

Until we see our work in this life as adventure, as going beyond the comfort zones of conventional acceptance, we may be missing what we came here to do.

In a television interview with Bill Moyers, now recorded in the book *The Power of Myth*, the world's foremost expert on mythology, Joseph Campbell comments that when you follow your bliss you start to live the life you are meant to be living.

> …you begin to meet people who are in the field of your bliss, and they open the doors to you. I say, follow your bliss and don't be afraid, and doors will open where you didn't know they were going to be.

It takes courage to step out into the wilderness, but there is help along the way. Divine Love guides our purpose and vision. When we claim our oneness with divine Love, we remember that this whole human experience is simply a script we are writing to mirror our highest awareness of the truth of our spiritual identity, our purpose is fulfilled. We don't have much choice. We must do what we came to do, and once we understand how we write our own life scripts, nothing can stop us from fulfilling our unique purpose and vision for this life.

Let go and trust

Dear Father Mother, what is the truth about me? I am your child, pure and perfect spirit and truth. I know everything I need to know to be joyful and happy. I know my selfhood in radiant goodness. I am not heavy and tired because my energy is the divine energy of Spirit and I am able to feel this energy always.

I am not resistant to good or fearful of discord in my life. My life is perfectly harmonious and is flowing effortlessly towards my higher good. What I affirm is my reality.

I manifest everything that is for my highest good. I claim my divine perfection now and am at ease in perfect unfolding. Everything is exactly as it should be in this moment. I am where the highest good can enter my experience. I am full of light, love and pure knowing. Discord is a lie about my being. I cannot be aging or unwell, lost, lonely or lacking.

I am in this moment simply reflecting all that I AM— eternal spring, perfect awareness and knowing, perfect companionship, and perfect abundance in everything I need to live from my highest good. I am not subject to illusion and fear. All that flows into my life is radiant joy and perfection.

Let go and flow with the peace and gentleness of perfection. This is my truth now and forever. Yes!!!!! This is my truth now and forever. Amen.

CHAPTER 13

BUT WHO AM I?

You are what you think.
All that you are arises from your thoughts.
With your thoughts you make your world.
Gautama Buddha

OUR ULTIMATE AIM MUST BE TO COME INTO FULL AWARENESS of our true identity as expressions of divine Love, God—to know only spiritual reality. However, we can only attain this awareness to the degree we live our growing understanding of the oneness of all creation in this world of physical form—which is, after all, our present highest perception of reality. Theory will not do it. Talking about the allness of Love and harmony and then living in judgment and condemnation of ourselves and others will not do it. We have already discussed that our identity is not to be found in the masks behind which we sometimes hide in order to protect ourselves. We are so much more than these masks. Our identity is not to be found in the trappings of our life—our various activities, possessions and jobs.

This current life experience is where we learn and practice our first lessons about spiritual reality, where we awaken to remember what is really true about us as spiritual beings. As we awaken to our spiritual identity, we naturally mirror it in the scripts we write for ourselves.

The remainder of this chapter was written for some young friends who wanted to know how answering the age-old question, "who am I?" could bring a greater sense of joy, freedom and peace to their lives.

But Who Am I?

But who am I? This can be a difficult question. Am I just a blob of matter with a mind inside that's on this planet along with umpteen other blobs of matter? Am I only here so long as I manage to stay alive?

This is a pretty depressing view of life if you believe it to be true. And yet for as long as man has been on this earth he has tried to find larger answers to this question, "who am I?"

Here is a dismal but amusing attempt to answer the question:

Probably

I guess therefore I am
or I might be
I really am not very sure
I think that I was what I was
but probably I'm not anymore

If I sat down and pondered the problem
the whys and the wherefores and such
it would be easy to see that I'm probably me
but I don't think it matters that much

But there again
on the other hand
and not really knowing what's what
amidst the confusion I've reached the conclusion
that it's probably true that I'm not.

Anonymous

We are all going to have to find our own answer to the question of "who am I"—an answer that satisfies us, that is our unique truth.

The answer I found that satisfied me as I grew up came from

the teachings of the Bible including the statement, "God created man in his own image." I felt very comfortable with the concept that I was actually the image of God. My comfort came from also having a clear idea of what or who God was to me, of what or of whom I was an image. If my concept of God had been a vengeful sky god figure then that wouldn't have been very comfortable.

While we need to see that each one of us is the full and complete expression of God, the talents we possess are our unique manifestations of that wholeness and completeness. We each have a particular purpose and role to play. I often think of a beautiful bouquet of my favorite varieties of flowers. Each type expresses its unique beauty, color, form, texture, and even blemishes. No single flower is better than another—each is different but still so perfectly lovely. That is like us. We don't need to be someone else because we each have our unique and special qualities. The worst thing we can do is to try to be someone else, because then we're not who we're supposed to be. The worst thing we can do is to try to be someone else because then we forfeit the expression of our own beauty in an attempt to mimic someone else's beauty.

Of course we can model the good qualities in others and always try to be better people but this is different from always wishing we were someone else.

I love this little story I found one morning in my cereal box.

On Being Yourself

You must learn that you cannot be loved by all people
You can be the finest apple in the world—ripe, juicy, sweet, succulent and offer yourself to all
But you must remember that there will always be people who don't like apples.
You must understand that if you are the world's finest apple and someone you love doesn't like apples, you have the choice of becoming a banana.
But you can always be the finest apple!
You must realize that if you become a second rate banana,

there will always be people who don't like bananas.
Furthermore, you can spend your life trying to become the
best banana which is impossible if you are an apple.
Or, you can try again to be the finest apple.

(Hubbards breakfast cereals)

We can really enjoy being different. We each express unique qualities of God effortlessly. For instance I love to share ideas with people. I like to talk—"no kidding" I hear my friends say. It's true—some qualities need taming! So I was drawn to a career as a public speaker and seminar presenter and not to a career as a librarian. It's not that one is better than the other. They're just different. And if we listen to our Father-Mother God's leading, we end up doing what we do best effortlessly.

Ask yourself, "what are my unique, strong, positive qualities?" Think, "what am I passionate about that blesses me and others? How can I most fully be the magnificent, unique person I really am?" And then listen carefully. Ask yourself, in line with your amazingly unique qualities, in what amazing and unique ways can you express your true self? When you discover how to be yourself you will find you can help others do the same. The ways you find to fully express your unique-ness will provide you with immeasurable joy and fulfillment while inspiring others to find their passionate purpose.

I love Marianne Williamson's thoughts on who we are (often at-tributed to Nelson Mandela) in *A Return to Love*:

> Our deepest fear is not that we are inadequate. Our deepest fear
> is that we are powerful beyond measure. It is our light, not our
> darkness, that most frightens us. We ask ourselves, who am I to
> be brilliant, gorgeous, talented and fabulous? Actually, who are
> you not to be? You are a child of God. Your playing small doesn't
> serve the world. There's nothing enlightened about shrinking
> so that other people won't feel insecure around you. We are all
> meant to shine, as children do. We were born to make manifest
> the glory of God that is within us. It's not just in some of us; it's
> in everyone. And as we let our light shine, we unconsciously give

other people permission to do the same. As we're liberated from our own fear, our presence automatically liberates others.

Enjoy discovering YOU!

A morning treatment for myself

Dear Father Mother Love, what is the truth about me right now? I am at the point of perfection right in this moment. Nothing but perfect good is unfolding and blossoming in my day. Great peace and calm are flowing over me, wrapping me in safety and protection.

The power of the Christ Truth is pouring into my consciousness to uplift and purify showing me all that is true and removing anything that is unlike good. There is no tension, no imbalance, no uncertainty, no frustration, not even any lack of love of Self or others. Because there is just one Mind, God, I am the evidence, the actioning of that Mind.

This Mind is Love and therefore I can only think and speak in perfect harmony and happiness. This Love Mind is all Life and therefore can be actioned in only what is harmonious and eternal. Because Life is God, the power, the atmosphere, the Allness of eternal Love, it cannot begin or end and it can never be anything less than vital Spirit.

"Let us feel the divine energy of Spirit bringing us into newness of life and recognize no power as able to destroy .... " this harmony (Mary Baker Eddy). Life is Spirit, Spirit is God, God is Love and Love is Mind. Therefore there is no mortal and material substance that can be inharmonious, limited, malfunctioning, growing up or growing down even, because there is no matter. The body and brain are simply thought projections and they are not who I truly am.

I am eternally spiritual and godlike and I live in vibrant joy and perfect spiritual knowing. I claim this now and I watch the results of this knowing unfold in ways beyond my wildest imaginings. Yes!!!!

CHAPTER 14

CHOOSING HOW WE WRITE OUR LIFE SCRIPTS

Go confidently in the direction of your dreams. Live the life you've imagined.
Henry David Thoreau

A FEW YEARS AGO I WAS HELPING A CLIENT CLARIFY HER SENSE OF direction in life. I was thinking about something she mentioned in an e-mail—how, after a conversation we had, she was inspired to put down some fresh thoughts about the protagonist in the screenplay she was writing. I thought how clearly she saw that she was creating this character, this screenplay, from her own inspiration, but did she see as clearly that she was also creating the screenplay of her own human life in the same way?

Do we see that we are writing the scripts for our own lives every time we make a choice? No, actually it is very likely that most of us do not see how accountable we are for everything that happens to us. Conventional wisdom has always taught us that we are at the mercy of God, heredity, chance, environmental and social expectations—that what happens in our lives is, for the most part, outside our control. Consequently, we can lay the blame for everything we don't like about our lives on someone else, on God, on the devil, on social customs, or on the weather even. As much as many people yearn for the security of following the certainty of conventional wisdom—the old dualistic edicts of what is right and what is wrong—in order to avoid being accountable for the choices they make, such predictability in life is disappearing fast.

We seem to have reached a point in this (r)evolution of consciousness when it is impossible to escape major choices about what we think and how we live our lives. As Mary Catherine Bateson puts it in *Composing a Life*, "Increasingly we will recognize the value in lifetimes of continual redefinition." Even those living within the confines of strict fundamentalist religious communities know by young adulthood that they may choose other ways to live and other philosophies in which to believe. Few are unaware that there are cultural belief systems other than the ones by which they live.

The effect of quantum physics' questioning whether matter is actually solid substance, has had major implications in how we now choose to think about reality. Religions like Christian Science have been healing effectively for over a century now—for instance, changing damaged matter into healthy matter simply with a change of thought. Such consistent healing has demonstrated that what we *think*, in fact, determines how reality looks to us. Do we believe what we see or do we see what we believe?

We all create our own reality whether we know it or not. What we choose to believe is up to us; we can create and re-create our reality in whatever ways we decide best serve us now. We determine what is and what is not going to be part of our experience every moment. Certainly the actual events may not be so consciously created as they are in the writing of a screenplay, but the expectations around the feelings we choose to live with surely are. And it is these *feelings*—dependencies and expectations—that determine our experiences.

Most of us are aware of how we choose to be happy or sad at any particular time. The same day, the same circumstances, the same people—what response are we going to elicit? While to some extent our response is conditioned by our personality—volatile, impatient, peaceful, accepting—the more we discover how we create our own reality the more control we have over how we want our lives to be.

As useful as this discovery of how we write our scripts is, and regardless of how many psychological techniques we master to become more self-aware— creative visualization, chanting, transcendental meditation, to name just a few—what we can achieve is still limited by the scope of our own perception of reality in this life. We simply create in physical form or symbols the thoughts and intentions that we hold in consciousness. If we believe, even subconsciously, that life is a tough struggle interspersed, hopefully, with brief moments of pleasure, then that is the way the events of our life will play out. The Bible verse, "That which I greatly feared, is come upon me," plays itself out when fear produces the very experience we fear most.

Conversely, when we believe that life is a joyful adventure, interspersed with some hard knocks every so often, this is what will play out for us. Because I know this with certainty for myself, many people comment that I am a great "manifester." For instance, because (at the time of writing this) I have had no home of my own for the last few years, I have moved several times. And yet each time when it becomes clear that it is time to move on, almost immediately I am offered a wonderful place to live. Not once in this time have I asked for a place to stay. The point is I *expect* to always manifest a sense of home, beauty, quiet and comfort wherever I am, and consequently I do.

I fully expect magnificent unfolding of good in my life and am somewhat surprised when I brush up against challenges. I know that actually I unconsciously script these challenges into my life drama because they represent the fears and blocks that I am holding onto in consciousness. I also know that these challenges give me the opportunity to confront the blocks and move beyond them, *if* I feel ready to, *if* I choose to. So in a sense I am still expecting good—I am looking for good in even the most challenging situation. I have an expectancy of good because much of the time I know that I am, in truth, a spiritual, divine being. To the extent I recognize this, I can write the script for my life to mirror this harmony.

So much is possible when we align ourselves with spiritual reality. Then we see beyond creating limiting scripts according to our perception of physical reality. We actually allow the Christ Truth or angel thoughts to reveal outcomes beyond anything our limited human consciousness could have imagined. With the help of this higher knowing, this Christ consciousness, we then become co-creators with God, writing spectacular scripts! The more we waken to our spiritual identity, the more alert we become to the choices we make. "Bad hair days" become choices. With such spiritual vision, the perspectives we choose can be made consciously.

Recently, I could have had a bad hair day. My laptop had crashed three weeks before and the computer company was still fiddling around with it. The laptop they'd lent me was so slow it really annoyed me. I felt as if I was in limbo. I spent much of the morning playing the victim—blaming others for my frustrations. I even blamed the weather, the house, anything I could think of. I was getting practically no writing done as my thoughts were well distracted.

Finally, I woke up with a laugh to what was going on. I asked my-self, "what if everything is exactly as it should be? What if the delay on my laptop is allowing me to take more reflective time, something that would certainly be beneficial, allowing me to focus on the "now?" By becoming aware of my attempt to use willpower to control events in my life, I immediately realized I could let go of outcomes and trust that good must unfold in its perfect timing. Tension and frustration would do nothing but stop my higher self from making love-centered choices.

I wrote in my journal, "See today that everyone is giving me exactly what I need when I need it. All is unfolding in perfect timing. Let go and know all is well." I forgot the frustrations and was soon writing productively and peacefully. The rest of the day was great.

A few years ago, I worked with a well-known architect who seemed to have written a highly successful life script for herself. But when Lynne came to see me she said she had spent thousands of dollars over many years trying to find a therapist who could help her deal with her inability to form long-term relationships. It seemed that whenever she got into a relationship she quickly became possessive, fearful of being abandoned, and would become verbally aggressive. In tears, she explained how just the week before, while driving home from a movie with her new boyfriend, he had mentioned he was going on a fishing trip with some friends for a few weeks. Immediately she thought it might just be an excuse to be away from her. She started hitting the dashboard and yelling at him, thereby bringing on the very situation she feared most. Her insecurities got the better of her and she exploded with fear. Her new boyfriend left her. Over the years, while therapists had spent months identifying her seemingly irrational behavior, the end result each time was merely to try to teach her how to manage her temper.

We spent three sessions talking about her spiritual identity as an expression of pure love. We talked about how, by identifying her spiritual nature, her human nature would naturally and effortlessly adjust to mirror her highest perception of truth. Lynne started to see that anger and instability were not part of her true nature, and that there was actually nothing to be afraid of. In any relationship she could trust that there would be the most perfect unfolding of harmony when she let go of trying to control outcomes.

As she came to see her spiritual identity and purpose were already in perfect harmony, Lynne released much of the fear and tension. She began to love the wonder of her individuality. Over the ensuing weeks she pondered the ideas we'd shared and since then has maintained a truly fulfilling long-term relationship. She is now writing a script for herself that includes great joy and freedom in relationship.

In her early years Lynne knew nothing about how she creates her own reality. Throughout years of therapy she learned more about her own accountability for the events in her life. Then, when she learned about her spiritual identity, she came to see that in the present moment she has full mastery of who she is and what she does. She can heal anything that no longer serves her. And she can make this life as magnificent as she can conceive it. In fact, she can make her life even more magnificent than she can conceive it once she knows that she co-creates with God, when she sees that the universal energy of Love is pouring into her consciousness lifting her to heights she has never even dreamed of. There is simply nothing and no one that can touch her joy, freedom and peace.

From this spiritual perspective, we could say that Love is writing our script in the sense that we are everything that this universal energy of Love is and we simply manifest our highest awareness of love consciousness. This knowing frees us to let go of thinking we need to outline what our ultimate joy, freedom and peace should look like. We surrender the need to control outcomes and instead trust that our human life must manifest our highest sense of perfect harmony in whatever ways it appears to us in tangible form.

The manifestation may come in the form of a red Ferrari because the Ferrari represents to us freedom, beauty and excitement. Equally, harmony may manifest in the form of a little hybrid car that fulfills our needs and our desire to preserve fossil fuels on the planet. We might realize harmony in the abundance of funds to purchase a new pair of running shoes because we prefer to be out in the fresh air and feeling fit. Perhaps harmony manifests in a fulfilling walk through nature when the consciousness of pure satisfaction over-rides our worries and we become perfectly satisfied with all the goodness in our lives.

Life can be utterly peaceful, it can be an exhilarating adventure, or it can be a combination of both—what I call active peace. Life can be exactly how we write our script to manifest our own unique perspectives. There is incredible freedom, satisfaction and abundance in this knowing.

How, then, do we write the script for our lives? By claiming the God-given spiritual qualities inherent in us as spiritual beings, and by expecting the manifestation of these qualities in our day-to-day lives. Instead of visualizing a red Ferrari, and thereby outlining the manifestation of our dream, we can understand that we possess perfect order, beauty and harmony, in our lives, and while a red Ferrari would certainly represent all these qualities, we are open to whatever is the highest manifestation of joy and freedom for us. There is great peace in such letting go, especially in letting go of the fears that would say we don't have enough—enough money, enough ability, enough spiritual knowing even. We have all we could ever need now because we are already perfect spiritual beings with infinite qualities of abundance, harmony, and joy. Knowing this is enough to jumpstart the manifestation of these qualities in our lives right now. Just remember that your human life simply represents what you hold in consciousness. We can co-create and re-design our life in harmony with God's spiritual design, in any manner we choose.

What does writing our own scripts have to do with clarifying our purpose and direction in life? Simply this: as we come to develop a deeply spiritual self-awareness and are attuned to the way our consciousness creates and evolves our life script at every moment, we are open to witnessing our highest sense of good unfolding naturally and effortlessly in our lives. We can make conscious choices that mirror our growing awareness of how we want our lives to be. We can make conscious choices that are love-centered, that allow us to live love and thereby enable us to discover our innate joy, freedom and peace more consistently.

As we are able to deal with our fears and limitations, our consciousness will be free to focus on what we want in our lives rather than on what we don't want. Our purpose will become clear as we discover what makes our heart sing and our eyes light up. We will know clearly what we love to do best and we will do it with such ease that our work will seem like play. Our passionate purpose might seem to be too much fun to be taken seriously but *fun* is exactly what Love is.

I love how Richard Bach, in *Bridge Across Forever*, describes the effect of such passion in what we love to do:

> Passionately obsessed by anything we love, an avalanche of magic flattens the way ahead, levels rules, reasons, dissents, bears us with it over chasms, fears, doubts. Without the power of that love we're boats becalmed on seas of boredom and those are deadly.

Passionate obsession or deadly boredom . . . put like that, the choice to find what we love to do and then do it for all we're worth, is certainly compelling.

But beware those little gremlins of doubt and fear—you know, the unjustified "should's" and the "ought to's"—the burdens of super-imposed obligations that we might confuse with our direction. It's okay. When we realize this whole life is a journey of exploration and discovery, the doubt and fear ultimately doesn't matter. We're learning just who our wild, vibrant, delightful being is! We're learning to love ourselves *just as we are* without the need for any other person's opinion or viewpoint. We must realize that others are on their own journey and that their journey doesn't look like ours. How could anyone else know what is right for us any more than we could know what is right for them? But we do know what is right for us when we listen to our heart.

It's important to remember that we're talking here about this very moment in our current human experience. The forever truth is that we are pure, eternal, spiritual beings, the evidence of Love itself, the evidence of the one all-knowing perfect Mind or intelligence, the evidence of Life that never starts and never stops. We are now, and always will be, *at the point of perfection.* One day we'll awaken fully to see this truth and our human experience will be gone from our consciousness, the only place it ever existed. We will no longer need to live in a world of physical form. In the meantime, even little glimpses of this truth of spiritual perfection heal. These glimpses allow us to manifest greater levels of harmony in our experience.

We are *co-creators with God.* Until we come to the true awareness of our perfect unity with God, we can remember that our thoughts determine our script. Therefore, we have the power to direct our thoughts in ways that not only increase our manifestation of abundance and unity, but also enable us to understand our identity and purpose as Love's expression. We can root out the falsity of perceived separation from Love, God. We decide the script because we are one with divine Love always. There is no separation. Just love— in which we not only find our joy, freedom and peace— but we live love, and love life.

Who you are

Never forget how incredible you are. You amaze me with your ability to accomplish what you do. And yet I should not be amazed. After all, it is because you know that there are no limits in this life except the ones you set for yourself or allow others to set for you. Because you know so clearly what it means to be the child of God, there is nothing, nothing at all that can limit you.

Your courage in being willing to try new things is so great—it is your key to freedom. With it you will conquer the highest peaks, and plumb the greatest depths to discover who you are, what you are to give to this world. Sure, you'll make mistakes, fall on your face sometimes, get criticized, even condemned, but this is your strength: to be willing to discover things for yourself and not just blindly accept the parameters that society and other people set.

Yes, you will cry often in your journey and you will often wonder whether it is all worth the fight. Deep down though, you know the old ways are not the life you seek. You will always be striving to make a difference, searching for treasure and meaning in your life. Remember that what you love to do, what fires your passion and joy in life, is what will be your greatest, your unique, gift to this world. Our Father-Mother God, divine Love, makes sure we love what she wants us to do.

I trust you will find and make plenty of time to laugh and love life, to glory in the richness and beauty all around you and to drink in the magnificence of who you are. Fly high today, or maybe just cruise, but whatever you do, remember how much you are loved, and this love is pouring into your soul, feeding and nourishing you even when you have no strength to do this for yourself. Unconditional love is forever.

CHAPTER 15

WAKING UP TO YOUR TRUE IDENTITY

We shall not cease from exploration
And the end of all our exploring
Will be to arrive where we started
And know the place for the first time

T.S. Elliot

BEFORE MOVING ON TO DISCUSS IN GREATER DETAIL HOW THE power of Love heals, I want to reiterate some of the key points from our discussion thus far on *Living Love*, on finding true joy, freedom and peace. Most important of all:

Do you know how perfectly amazing you are? Not just average, not below average, but completely and exquisitely phenomenal? Utterly unique —unable even to be compared to anyone else. Yes? No? If not, maybe you've still not thought about it enough. So let's think about it now.

Do you see what it means to be the immortal, spiritual, perfect expression or evidence of divine Love, perfect consciousness? It means that, in truth, you are everything Love is. You possess every quality that is part of perfect harmony. This means you are vital, dynamic, ageless, creative, wise, beautiful, peaceful, utterly glorious loveliness. Your perfect true selfhood is eternal and this selfhood is entirely unique, just as your fingerprints are entirely unique to you. There will never be another set of fingerprints exactly like yours. And there will never be another you. There is a place in the spiritual jigsaw puzzle of creation that can only be filled by you.

As you start to wake to spiritual, true identity, think of all the things that make you entirely unique and completely loving, lovely and lovable. Nothing else is possible. Draw a thought portrait of your-self that includes all the qualities you express as the child of God, the child of Love. You'll only just be scratching the surface of who you are but it'll be a start.

But what about the human self you think is very far from such loveliness? This self is really just like a thought projection, something we've created from a limited perception or awareness of who we re-ally are—as if we've forgotten who we are as spiritual beings. Writing at the end of the 19th century, Mary Baker Eddy saw this clearly when she wrote:

"Everything is as real as you make it, and no more so. What you see, hear, feel, is a mode of consciousness, and can have no other reality than the sense you entertain of it."

But, some people would say, we didn't dream up the way we are. We came into the world this way. Consider the possibility that the thoughts of our parents, grandparents, and passively accepted world beliefs about chance, environment, heredity and so on, conspired to present us this way to human consciousness, to the material senses. To the five physical senses, the way we are conditioned to believe is the way we appear as a physical body with a limited mind inside it. But as Eddy continues:

"It is dangerous to rest upon the evidence of the senses, for this evi-dence is not absolute, and therefore not real, in our sense of the word."

Once we become aware that the human body is simply a com-plex thought projection, we have complete control over the results. In human consciousness we choose what we want to hold onto and in this way write our own scripts. This process may include popular psychological methods such as the power of positive thinking, but writ-ing our own scripts is really much more than this. It includes the aware-ness of our dominion as spiritual beings over this whole human ex-perience.

Quantum physics also tells us something about how we write our own scripts, observing that even the intention of a scientist can alter the results of an experiment. In *Leadership and the New Science*, Margaret Wheatley explains how some physicists have given up

> ... searching for things finite and discrete because, as they experimented to find elementary particles, they found "things" that changed form and properties as they responded to one another, and to the scientist observing them.... If quantum matter develops a relationship with the observer and changes to meet his or her expectation, then how can there be scientific objectivity? If the scientist structures an experiment to study wave properties, matter behaves as a wave. If the experimenter wants to study particles, matter obliges and shows up in particle form....once the observers chooses what to perceive, the effect of perception is immediate and dramatic.

What do we choose to perceive about ourselves?

Wheatley's book is useful in understanding something about how science and spirituality are closing ranks in an attempt to understand identity in a new way.

Continuing the earlier quotation about creating our own reality, Eddy says:

"All that is beautiful and good in your individual consciousness is permanent. That which is not so is illusive and fading."

What are we going to choose to believe about ourselves? If we accept anything less than our beauty and goodness we're getting lost in the illusion that we are not the children of God. We're getting lost in the dream that there are two beings—a perfect spiritual being that is our true selfhood and then a separate, physical self that we kick in the shins because it's not perfect.

I've discovered a very interesting trend in my healing practice. Many people who seem to understand these ideas about spiritual perfection and how we write our own scripts in this human life get stuck when it comes to healing. I find they can accept the concept that matter is a subjective, fleeting state of consciousness, and therefore ultimately unreal in the context of spiritual consciousness, and, furthermore, that physical illness in the spiritual context is actually impossible. Yet they think they have to go through a process to change consciousness, to change their existing identity. They believe it is necessary to become better spiritual thinkers, better people, kinder, more loving people, or that they have to study and learn more. They believe a process is required before they can feel their spiritual perfection and therefore witness healing.

While it is true that at some point in time we must all throw off the shackles that bind us to hurtful, limiting behaviors, this will naturally happen as we recognize that such behaviors prevent us from experiencing the higher joy, freedom and peace natural to us as spiritual beings. This is part of the awakening from a dream state of physical limitation.

Healing happens the instant we glimpse our physical reality as simply a dreamstate and nothing more. In truth, how can there be any process of healing if we are *already* at the point of spiritual perfection? When we glimpse for one instant that we already have a perfect spiritual selfhood that never deteriorates or disappears, we experience healing of whatever the less-than-perfect thought held in consciousness was. The dream is eliminated. Our human life then mirrors the divine.

Healing or harmonizing in this way does not mean there isn't plenty to learn on our journey from the human perception to the spiritual reality. Blind faith or positive thinking will not get us to the point of consistently glimpsing reality. Understanding our own identity as the evidence of God consciousness and the practical living of love and harmony are both needed. In fact, living love moment by moment helps us understand what it means to be the essence and expression of Love. We simply can't practice what we don't understand.

Neither can we put our heads in the sand and pretend this human existence—our present reality—doesn't exist. For the moment, this perception of reality does exist and it is the school yard of our learning and practice. For instance, in order to understand our spiritual relationship to Love we need to continually practice loving kindness. We need to get beyond relying solely on intellectual reasoning and pay attention to feelings and emotions—the signposts of the heart and soul—that show us *how* to live love. We can't just talk about being loving. Intellect alone isn't sufficient.

Our focus must be to celebrate our spiritually perfect and true selves, the unique and amazing spiritual beings we really are. When I celebrate my true self I find that my consciousness effortlessly fills with all that is beautiful and good and whatever healing needs to happen in order to mirror such harmony in my human life happens naturally. In other words, I have found that my experiences in this life effortlessly mirror the divine. It's true for all of us. We find ourselves expressing our true spiritual identity, our higher love consciousness. And as we wake up to this true, utterly exquisite and unique identity we discover a phenomenal life purpose that, not surprisingly, includes living love.

Just who you are

You say, "but this is just who I am"

*(A small somewhat insignificant being with so many
limits, faults, fears and doubts.
Quite invisible to the world, really.)*

*But this is not who you are
No, this is not who you are*

*You amaze me with who you are
You are so beautiful and graceful
But that's not all who you are*

*You are so smart and wise
But that's not all who you are*

*You are so deeply spiritual and open to guidance
But that's not all who you are*

*You are so spontaneous and joyful
But even that is not all who you are*

*Sometimes you are also erratic and unpredictable and wild and angry
and defeated and sad and frustrated and irrational and lost and lonely.
Sometimes you are so critical of yourself, so intolerant, so unforgiving. And
sometimes you are unsure of your path, unsure of what you have done,
what you are about to do, what you are doing right now.
But that's not all who you are*

*You fly high and range wide in search of your truth
others can join you, walk hand in hand, share your journey
as you share theirs—supporting each others' dreams and delights
as you support your own – forgiving your mistakes, loving who you are
being, who you are becoming*

(more)

*But you cannot be put in a box, confined, made to conform
to someone else's vision for you if it is not your own*

And even all this—this is not all who you are

*You are not just what you do—all the amazing things, all the silly
things, all the spontaneous things, all the nonsensical things, all the
smart things, all the go-nowhere things*

*You are an incredible kaleidoscope of creativity and uniqueness
Something so stunning in its brilliance that sometimes the Universe
stops just to watch you
In awe of your courage and your vision for what is possible*

*You are something so humble and quiet and gentle
that you seem to tiptoe through this world*

*This world in awe of your commitment to be YOU
In awe of your courage to BE*

*A world that celebrates, as I do, this amazing being you are
All who you are
Just as you are*

PART FOUR

THE POWER OF LOVE TO HEAL

CHAPTER 16

SOME TRUTHS FUNDAMENTAL TO HEALING:

The Allness of God, Good
The Perfection of Spiritual Man
The Nothingness of Evil
The Illusion of Matter

IN ORDER TO HEAL WHATEVER IS DISCORDANT IN OUR LIVES, IT IS necessary to understand ourselves as spiritual beings. It is necessary to understand our relationship to our Father-Mother God, divine Love, and to know that this power of Love is all that exists. In other words, there is no power of evil or discord—no "devil" that can sabotage our innate harmony. Neither is matter anything other than a thought projection—a part of our present belief that we are limited, physical beings trapped in a space/time dimension.

Understanding something about the four fundamental truths I talk about in this chapter is a first step in writing scripts for our human lives that mirror our inner truth. This understanding is also vital to healing physical and emotional problems we may face. First articulating and then understanding these concepts enables a natural adjustment of our lives toward the reflection of a harmony that flows from our deep inner knowing, from our hearts and souls. We call this healing but in reality it is simply waking to remember our spiritual nature as the very evidence of Love, awakening to what is already true—our present perfection.

i) The Allness of God, Good

How do you describe or articulate the God concept? What or who is God? Each of us may have a different definition. For some, the word God is very precious. For others the word Love conveys their sense of the Almighty. Others, who have grown up with a concept of God with which they cannot identify, have abandoned the whole idea of a governing Principle or God. Others, for whom the word God has always had a very masculine connotation, like to combine the concepts of the God and Goddess—God denoting the masculine leading and guiding qualities, and Goddess the feminine, nurturing, intuitive aspects. Still others prefer the term the Universe. I like the term, the universal energy of Love. Some refer to he, others she, others it. I use all these ideas and terms interchangeably simply because words can't even begin to define a feeling and knowing that is indefinable.

Central to consistent metaphysical healing in the way I know and practice it is the understanding that God is All. What does that mean? It means that *all that God is, is all that there is.* And that includes us. Just as the sun would be nothing without its rays, so too God cannot exist separate from his expression. He would be unexpressed. Nothing exists apart from the oneness of God and his creation. There is no separation in oneness.

This idea of the inseparability of God and his expression, his creation, is a difficult concept to grasp if we try to hold to the idea that God is some sort of super-human or spiritual being who watches over us and controls our day-to-day human lives. But if we can imagine God as an atmosphere or power of harmony, as a principle maintaining perfect balance and order in all creation, this helps us obtain a sense of God that enables us to understand why healing can occur. Think of the principle of mathematics. There are certain foundational principles essential to solve equations; simple things learned early such as $2+2=4$ are required before the student may advance to learn calculus. Without an understanding of these basics the whole science of mathematics would be flawed. In the same way, understanding the basic laws of God and man—the allness of the power of Love and the

nothingness of matter or any apparent opposing power of discord—
is essential to spiritual, metaphysical healing.

Using the much-abused word God to define this all-powerful
principle of harmony is not a requirement. One of the greatest difficulties we face in trying to describe spiritual ideas is the lack of suit-
able language to do so. As I said in an earlier chapter, the English language has just one word, "love," to convey many different meanings.
The Inuit language, on the other hand, provides at least thirty two
separate words for identifying these different degrees or aspects. I'm
told there is even a word that would deal with "I love you but I
wouldn't want to go seal hunting with you!"

In the Aramaic language spoken by Jesus, the word for "love" as
in "love your enemies," has a different degree of intensity than that
used in "I love you."

Considering the difficulty of using a limited language to explain
spiritual concepts, I find it helpful, as I said earlier, that the teachings
of Christian Science provide seven synonyms for the word God, each
of which identifies an aspect of who or what God is: Life, Truth, Love,
Principle, Mind, Soul and Spirit.

God is Spirit. Therefore if God is All and he/she is Spirit then
everything is spirit and spiritual. This idea of God is very different
from the traditional sky god of historical Christianity: a God that is
aware of our human lives, our strengths and weaknesses, our actions
and thoughts, and the being who ultimately assigns us to heaven or
hell when we die. The God with whom I can identify is a power rather
than a sort of super-being. I often think of this power as being like
the atmosphere in which we live—invisible yet everywhere present,
and in which and of which we *are*.

So if God is Spirit and God is All, we can reason that we are
entirely spiritual simply because All *and* something else is an impos-
sibility. Using such reasoning, what are the implications for matter?
Quite literally, earth-shattering. The consequences of this thinking
are leading many quantum physicists to the same conclusion: matter
is non-existent, merely a concept we are conditioned to believe is solid
and tangible. Some physicists are beginning to say that everything,
including us, is, in fact, a form of energy.

The allness of Spirit is also Love. Therefore Love is all there is, harmony is all there is. Everything real is harmonious because everything real is an outcome of love. The appearance or evidence of anything inharmonious—discord, sickness, decay, even death—is part of the script we write, the projection of our own thoughts of limitation or what might be called, according to the Bible story, the Adam dream. In the Adam and Eve story it is interesting to note that God is supposed to have put Adam into a deep sleep. The story, which never mentions Adam waking up, tells us a lot about the dream state from which we are only now beginning to awaken.

We can also describe or define this spiritual power of Love as the one Mind, the ever-present eternal wisdom or intelligence that knows all that is true. We live in the atmosphere of intelligence, in our true state, always knowing what is real, always aware of the higher reality of perfect God and perfect man, spiritual and eternal.

This power of infinite wisdom is also the one power of all Life and in this Life everything is eternal, ageless, never born and never dying, never growing up or growing down, never budding, never deteriorating. Life is active, moving, emitting, always held at the point of perfection.

This power of ageless and eternal Life is the one Truth and the one Soul or creative power of *All That Is*, radiating beauty and vibrancy. This Soul consciousness is dynamic, holding all in perfect balance and harmony because it is the one Principle of all.

Just Oneness

I am dynamic, vibrant, centered, joyful spirit, the complete consciousness of all good. Nothing comes from outside my consciousness. There are no external experiences —all is within me. I am not dependent on people, places, processes, or chance. God is the provider of all that is, because she is Life, Love, Principle, Truth, Spirit, Mind and Soul.

Nothing unlike good can enter my experience because good is all. Discord, dysfunction, dis-ease, disturbance are illusions, part of the lie that there is a power apart from Good, that matter is real, that there is some sort of evil power that can disrupt my joy and completeness and happiness. This lie is simply the delusion that the pure, perfect, joyful, vibrant, delighted and delightful I AM, God, is not all, that there is good and then something else.

When this delusion is seen for what it is—a lie—it disappears into its native nothingness effortlessly, fully and finally. I am one with Love. I am one with Life. I include all joy. I am complete in oneness.

ii) The Perfection of Spiritual Man

Suppose you wanted to paint the concept of beauty, what would you paint? Suppose you wanted to paint the idea of joy or the quality of peace, or even perfection? Each one of us would paint these concepts in so many utterly unique ways according to our own perception or inspiration.

God, the one infinite power of divine Love, creates or paints his creation—each of us—as unique, perfect and pure blends of spiritual qualities such as strength, persistence, harmony, joy, intelligence and beauty.

These qualities are painted in the picture of spiritual perfection and are always in perfect balance. Sensitivity is balanced with courage and strength, peace and calm are balanced with laughter and fun. The ability to give is balanced with the ability to receive, the grace to love others is balanced with the grace to love ourselves. Because infinite Love, God, is the only power that exists, each one of us must be painted in perfect loveliness.

What must the truth be about the human mind and body that appears to us as a mix of good and bad, prone to imbalance—too old or too young, too much sensitivity or too much aggression, too much imperfection and too many problems? Is this the picture of God's creating? No. Our paintings, detailing the limitations of the human dream, are inverted images of the truth about us. This inversion is described at the start of the Bible where it says that God created man in his own image. As God is all good and entirely spiritual, man must also be all good and spiritual. As just mentioned, the second chapter of Genesis begins with what may be seen as an allegory, the Adam and Eve story of the downfall of man. God puts man into a deep sleep, and in this deep sleep, this dream state, man is disobedient and God banishes him from the Garden of Eden. If God has created man in his image, the second version of man's creation can be nothing more than a way of explaining what appears to happen when we lose sight of spiritual reality, when mass consciousness forgets what is true and paints its own version of reality.

The delusion of collective world consciousness is pervasive and very convincing. We can get trapped into painting pictures according to what current world thought sees as fashionable or trendy. Thin, blonde, straight hair, rock star, rich and famous. Are these the main ingredients in the recipe for joy and harmony? If we think appearance and possessions alone are sufficient we'll eventually be in for a rude awakening. Harmony in our lives comes from harmony in our thinking. If our thinking starts with an abundance of loving thoughts—kindness, care, consideration, gentleness and so on—the unfolding of our life experiences will similarly express abundance in all things that make us happy and peaceful. Success and wealth may be present in our lives but they will surface as a result of our kindness and care for others rather than as the result of greed and power games. Whatever forms our abundance takes, our lives will pattern the divine.

The dream of mortality or limited world thought ultimately cannot trap us into believing any negative qualities or physical characteristics about ourselves. We have a choice as to what we accept. We can choose to accept the world picture painted of us, faults and all. Or we can choose to see the picture of God's creating, painted in glorious technicolor, radiating joy-filled laughter and perfect balance—spiritual, just as God sees us.

Very often this is not easy. For a very long time I thought of myself as much less than perfect, in fact as rather unlovable. No matter that other people loved me; I saw my imperfections and faults and I dwelled on them so much that they were very real to me. With this focus I simply could not appreciate or even believe what other people saw in me. I let myself get fooled into believing I was a physical being out of balance, subject to chance, heredity, environment, and so on.

Then I began to wake up to see this was not a picture I wanted to accept of myself. I saw that I was actually a unique blend of the glorious spiritual qualities of infinite Love, Soul, God. This was the picture I was going to recognize and see painted before me because this is how God sees me—full of joy, beauty, balance, harmony, wisdom, peace, strength, courage, goodness, purity and perfection. Each day I am erasing the faded lines of a falsely painted picture, thereby enabling me to see the glorious lines of God's painting. And because

I am always co-creating with God, I am adding to this painting, and writing my own script with new inspiration each day. Each day I love myself more. I love being me. And with this love of me comes a greater and greater outpouring of love for all mankind. Loving ourselves and others in this way is an integral part of living love.

You too can witness your painting of spiritual perfection, each day made more beautiful with fresh inspiration. Herein lies your promise of freedom.

A close friend of mine phoned me a while ago, feeling, he said, lost in a maze of limiting perceptions about himself. He is someone who has a deep spiritual wisdom and a great ability to help other people discover their spiritual identity, and yet he felt as if he was becoming more and more engulfed in what he knew was just a part of the human dream. It seemed he could not get his feelings to align with this knowing. He had felt very unhappy for a long time.

I felt such a flood of love pour out to him, particularly as I had been lost in a similar state of self-doubt and criticism. I emailed the following treatment to him, and it helped break the limiting dream that had somehow mesmerized him for so long. While, like me, he continues to work on understanding the truth of who he is as the very evidence of divine Love, like me, he has never again been gripped by such debilitating self-condemnation. This freedom and peace of mind is waiting for each one of us as we wake up to our true spiritual identities and to remember who we actually are.

Discovering your magnificence

What is the truth about you, dear Friend? You are Love's radiance. Nothing else can claim a place in your consciousness because Love is all. The lies of the false ego consciousness are illusions and fade into oblivion when this truth of Love's allness is glimpsed.

Even when this bad dream threatens to engulf you, just remember that it has never been the truth of who you are, and it never will be. Dearest Light Being, you are always held at the point of perfection, singing and dancing and loving, far above and beyond this mortal dreamscape, forever in a place of spiritual light and heart-felt joy.

For now, you choose to hold to this human experience as your truth, but remember it is only a dream. Each time you awaken even just a little to remember who you truly are and where you truly live, you are able to live the dream with more lightness, with more lightheartedness, and with a growing realization of the transience of this dream.

Dear Friend, feeeel a gentle flow of peace enfolding you right in this moment. Be very still. So still that you can feel yourself wrapped in Love's arms. You can feel yourself immersed in a moment of eternal bliss, a moment repeating itself for eternity. This is the law of your perfect being. Your ability to see the law of Love in action is inevitable as you claim your spiritual magnificence right now. And if in this moment you have forgotten how to feel this magnificence, then I am doing it for you. I am wrapping you in such powerful bliss that you are becoming intoxicated by its heaven scent. You are powerless to fight the inevitable slide into pure joy. Ah yes, now you are remembering and you are unfolding your wings of light to soar high above the dream.

So much exhilaration as you fill to overflowing with the beauty and rapture of such divine perfection that you are becoming a pure channel for Love's outpouring to all beings. And not really becoming—you have always been this pure channel of Love. This is your real selfhood as Love's expression. You are simply awakening from the deep sleep of this dream to remember your divine perfection. Yes!!

iii) The Nothingness of Evil

One of the criticisms of the idea that we are, in truth, always at the point of perfection and always the evidence, the image of the one infinite Spirit or power of divine Love, is that it is unrealistic to say we don't have a shadow side. The shadow side is where our fears reside, where anger, intolerance and ignorance exist. Yes, in this human experience it would be true to say we do have a shadow side.

Again, we need to distinguish between the absolute truth of our present spiritual perfection—the understanding of which enables us to heal and to live in ever increasing harmony, joy and freedom—and this human experience. In this dream we do appear to experience a shadow side, the side that we are setting out to unsee.

A shadow is a useful example to explain the concept of a perceived discordant state of thought in this life of physical form. For instance a shadow only occurs when a light source is blocked by something. The shadow appears in the shape of whatever is interrupting the light flow. The shadow is not an actual substance but simply an area of the absence of light.

In the human dream experience where we do not understand or remember the truth of our spiritual perfection as spiritual beings created by Love to exactly image forth harmony, we create a block. This block forms the shadow side that believes in, even expects, the inevitability of discord and inharmony as part of our experience. So long as we create this block to the light of Love, we create an area of lack of light, and as soon as we dissolve the block, the light pours back in.

There is a story about a man who asks some friends to help him remove the darkness from a hole. To his friend Wind he says, "Blow in the hole and blow out the darkness." Wind blows furiously, but nothing happens. Then the man says to his friend Rain, "Pour your water in the hole and flood out the darkness." Rain tries all day but nothing happens. He tells Thunder, "Please make your loud noise and blast the darkness out!" Thunder booms and crashes with loud claps and distant rumbles and, again, nothing happens. Finally, exasperated, the man goes to his friend, Light and says, "I beg you, go shine the darkness out of the hole." Light goes down into the hole and returns confused, declaring, "What are you talking about? There is no darkness there."

This story serves to remind us that to light and love, there is only light and love. This is the understanding that heals.

How can the sun see darkness? It cannot. How can a beam of light from the sun have a shadow? It cannot. Can you imagine an idea having a shadow? No, it doesn't have any solid state to block the light. Just so, in truth, a spiritual being cannot have a shadow side because she is pure good, the image, the light, of Love.

Never less than magnificent

I think I am not well. I have really just forgotten for the moment that I am not actually a material body that can get sick. I am the radiant magnificence of perfect Spirit. Such magnificence cannot be subject to discord, stress, weather, contagion or inharmony of any sort. Because I always am and always will be at the point of pure perfection I cannot really suffer from the illusion that I am a material body with a mind inside. No. I am

the eternal, ageless, vibrant living of LIFE
the joyful, funfilled, laughing and loving radiance of LOVE
the tender, gentle, caring, creative, child-like expression of SOUL
the pure and wise all-knowing clarity of MIND and TRUTH
the effortlessly ordered and effective evidence of PRINCIPLE
the manifestation of perfectly free and lovely SPIRIT.

I am surrounded by, and immersed in, infinite eternal perfection; exquisite beauty in even the tiniest flowers, leaves, sunbeams and raindrops.

I see what so many people can't even believe in. I see magnificence because I am that magnificence. I see a whole world, a whole universe of breathtaking, heart-stopping, mind-dancing glory because I am that glory. I am simply seeing the evidence of my own beautiful and tender, glorious dream. I remember that I am the center of that dream, the author of every bit of beauty, love and joy that I see. I am the creator of my universe of perfection.

How impossible then for me to be anything less than equally perfect, free, harmonious and joy-filled. When I fill my beautiful consciousness with forgiveness, love, and appreciation for this perfect, radiant, spiritual being that I am, the illusions of discord, discomfort and limitation will simply fade into nothingness "like dew before the morning sunshine" (Mary Baker Eddy).

Let go, dear self, and just love, love, love. Love my self first and foremost. Keep me tucked up in forgiving, gentle, tender love and watch the illusion disappear. This illusion was only ever real in thought so when it loses its power to seem real, when there is no room for it in thought any more, it will be gone. I will think I have been healed but really I will have awakened to what has always been true—my forever spiritual perfection.

iv) The Illusion of Matter

I have just received a phone call from a young woman who is on a business trip away from home and feeling very ill and desperate. I am lost in thought wondering what is really going on in her mental and emotional world in this moment. I am praying for Love's guidance to help me see her as she has always been and always will be—perfect and complete as a spiritual being held in the arms, the power, of divine Love. She is not a mortal body with a limited mind inside subject to chance, environment, contagion, tension, discord, or illness. She is a divine being, the manifestation of all that God, Love, Life, Mind, Truth, is, always at the point of spiritual perfection. Even just a glimpse of this knowing is enough to annihilate the lie of life in matter.

As I sit at my desk lost in thought and gazing out the window, I am suddenly aware of my own image staring back at me. With a storm raging all day, the night has drawn in early. Instead of the usual vista of deep green redwoods and patches of sky beyond, all I see is a dark misty background and my own image reflected back at me. As I gaze at myself I see the trees through me. I see that I am a rather transparent image, a suggestion of solid form, a projection, merely a reflection. And yet is this not perhaps a better representation of who I am, than this apparently solid body sitting in the chair? Looking at this image I see clearly the unique "me" that is most important—the qualities that, all mixed together, make me unique. I see, reflecting back, humor, vitality, sensitivity, deep spiritual knowing, laughter, tears, spontaneity, patience, stubbornness, impatience, bravery, fear, supreme optimism, timid caution, a lioness, a mouse. Ah yes, what fun! All this and no solid matter to go with it—just a suggestion of form.

I see this is true of my client. She is also a complete spiritual being composed of a unique mix of feelings and qualities. How can an idea ever be subject to chance and dissolution? Once an idea is thought up, it will never cease to exist. In the same way the color blue may be thought of by an infinite number of people for eternity, but the idea of blue can never cease to exist. As the one Creator of all is pure Love, Love can only think up—create—lovely thoughts. Each of Love's ideas or expressions is forever intact and is immune to the dream of life in matter, the dream of discord as a part of living, or the suggestion that matter is real.

Right now in this perfect moment nothing exists beyond Truth. Matter is a concept of thought. The realization of the spiritual perfection of creation transforms the human into a higher expression of this perfection. The human mirrors the divine when we glimpse the truth of perfection.

And isn't that all that matter is—merely a suggestion of form affected entirely by the intention of the person perceiving it? As I explain in an earlier chapter, according to some quantum physicists, matter responds differently according to what is being held in consciousness. Physicist Amit Goswami, in his book, *The Self-Aware Universe: how consciousness creates the material world*, shares many valuable insights. Goswami attempts to bridge the gap between science and spirituality. While there are many areas of divergence between his concept of reality and mine, Goswami argues that consciousness creates all there is. Consciousness is the only reality—something transcendental, outside of space-time, non-local, and all pervading. While Goswami doesn't use the word God, maintaining this word is too limiting, his explanation fits well with the way I use the word, or its synonym, divine Love. In fact, they are one and the same, the only reality, the one Mind that is God and that man expresses. Just a glimpse of this truth of Oneness transforms the way we live our lives.

Goswami concludes that this mystical truth, this "nothing-but-consciousness" must be experienced in order to be truly understood. This is what healing is all about—being able to distinguish between reality and illusion.

My client? She called shortly to say she was making a rapid recovery. Of course she was. The truth of her spiritual identity had been uncovered, and the dream of discord was dismissed as having no lasting effect on her whatever. The Christ Truth, or Love's angel thoughts, had come to both of us uplifting and waking us to remember what was true about her spiritual identity.

Healing is not affected by time or distance. Neither does healing require physical touch. It makes no difference whether the healer and patient are separated by thousands of miles. Healing is not a process of learning, of getting from A to Z, although it may seem that way in our three dimensional perception of life. Healing is simply remembering our forever, spiritual perfection.

The following affirmation is a good one to read before drifting off to sleep at night. Think of it as a practice exercise in self-healing.

Resting in love

And what tonight? Love's child held in love. What else is possible? There is no discordant experience other than in the illusory dream of matter. The dream has nothing to do with my true and only selfhood. Right now, as I drift off to sleep let me feel enveloped in a gentle glow of sweet, tender love. Let me feel Love's arms holding me, restoring my energies, nurturing my being, filling my dreams with loving and lovely images of beauty and goodness as I sleep so quietly and deeply. There is no sadness, no disappointment, no hurt anywhere in my God consciousness, my Love consciousness. Right now all I can feel is coming to me from the one Source of all good, enfolding me in perfect gentle knowing and tenderness.

Dear God, you are All that Is—all Goodness, Light, Love and perfect Harmony. And I am your perfect expression, possessing everything beautiful and good, peaceful and gentle, joyful and loving. I sleep in your arms, safe and still. Thank you.

CHAPTER 17

HEALING THE BODY

Consciousness constructs a better body when faith in matter has been conquered.

Mary Baker Eddy

WRITTEN OVER A CENTURY AGO, THE ABOVE STATEMENT HAS always intrigued me. It was written in *Science and Health* long before quantum mechanics proposed, as discussed already, that matter is not the solid reality it has always been considered to be. Having healed herself and many others by what she called "affirming the truth and denying the error"—affirming the truth of our spiritual reality, and denying the error of believing in an oftentimes discordant physical reality—Eddy became convinced, as had the Buddha, that matter is simply an illusion. As she put it, "Sooner or later we shall learn that the fetters of man's finite capacity are forged by the illusion that he lives in body instead of in Soul, in matter instead of in Spirit."

Eddy was certain it was this understanding of the nothingness of matter, coupled with Jesus' realization of the allness of Love—of God as Love—that had enabled him to heal so effectively. When Jesus said, "He that believeth on me, the works that I do shall he do also; and greater works than these shall he do; because I go unto my Father," he had obviously expected that others would continue to heal after he was no longer on this earth plane.

While the Christian church established itself around Jesus' teachings, the ability to heal as Jesus and his disciples had done was lost by

300 AD, no doubt submerged under doctrinal teachings that had forgotten the importance of living love as the basis of healing.

Many mystics, saints and prophets over the centuries have been able to heal by understanding the allness of spiritual reality and the power of unconditional love. As we are able to live in harmony with compassion and non judgment, we all have this same ability to heal effectively anything that doesn't fit with such harmony and anything that is discordant in our lives and in the lives of those around us. The ability to heal the body becomes as normal an expectation as does healing of relationship, financial, or psychological problems.

Once we understand the unreality of matter in some capacity, even though we still accept this life of physical form as our present reality, our consciousness mirrors the divine and our bodies naturally become more harmonious in their functions and capacities. Matter manifests our expectations and those of collective world consciousness. This is what we call our human life. Our human life is the acting out of our evolving consciousness. It is our thought projections made manifest. The more our conscious awareness of a higher spiritual reality evolves, the more this physical form of life will continue to evolve into greater freedom and harmony. In effect, once we become conscious of this process we will re-write our scripts to mirror the divine.

The God consciousness—the universal energy of Love—is not, however, cognizant of this so-called physical reality we have created for ourselves. Human "reality" is our creation. Once we assume this God consciousness as our own, our perception of reality will change to see only spiritual reality. We will no longer need to construct any body for ourselves because we will have moved beyond the need for a physical form of identity. Our self-aware love consciousness will expand until it embraces and becomes a part of the entire oneness of Love.

We need to remember that we are always evolving; we are moving closer to remembering our ultimate love consciousness which has always been present. When we obtain even just the briefest hint of how immersion in this love consciousness feels, we find our life experiences naturally merge into greater harmony. We call this healing but it is, in fact, just an adjustment of perception. In this moment of love consciousness we see through the eyes of love, we expect to see harmony. When we *expect* to see harmony, we do.

When I give a healing treatment, when I un-see the lie of a discordant situation and therefore "treat" consciousness, I usually go through the process of affirming what is true about my client as a perfect and complete spiritual expression of Love, and of denying what is untrue about them as a limited physical being. Most importantly, though, I try to immediately get to a feeling of calm stillness. This feeling is part of my love consciousness that knows clearly that all is well. My love consciousness knows there is nothing but love, only the oneness of love in which there can be no separation, discord or disease. In that moment I *feel* this to be true. I feel a quiet, absolutely unquestioning certainty. When I get to this feeling I know the healing adjustment in my client's perception has occurred. The finishing touch is a spontaneous feeling of bubbling up joy and—an almost inevitable smile. Then I know my work is finished. The point is, we can't quantify this feeling. We can't learn it through knowledge, logic or intellect. It just *is*.

Once when my youngest child was only about three months old, she became ill with a very high temperature. She was so lethargic that, despite my best efforts to affirm the truth about her true spiritual identity and deny the evidence that she was a sick little baby, I became quite frightened. As I was unable to bring about a quick healing, I bundled Debbie up and drove to the office of the doctor who had delivered her. Dr. Tim Smart had been so impressed by the rapid and completely painless delivery I had experienced (it had been this way with all my children), that he had a strong regard for what spiritual healing could accomplish.

As he examined Debbie he showed serious concern and suggested that under normal circumstances she should certainly be admitted to a hospital immediately. I can't tell you now what he said was wrong with her because I know almost nothing about different diseases. I have learned that the less I hold medical information in thought, the less authority I give the problem in consciousness. Medical diagnoses are, for me, simply opportunities to adjust a picture of discord to one of harmony, regardless of what the symptoms might be. Healing a sore finger or healing a fever are both a matter of changing a picture of discord to one of harmony. One condition is no more serious than another unless we give either condition greater power in our own thinking.

After telling me what was wrong with Debbie and that it was a complicated problem that might result in several weeks in hospital, the doctor suggested that before resorting to medical intervention, I take her home again for the rest of the day and continue to pray. "Because I've seen what you can do when you pray, I know she will be so much better off if you can heal this quickly," he said. As he ushered me out of his office he asked me to call him in a few hours with a progress report.

I remember leaving his office feeling light and uplifted. Dr. Smart had been so kind and compassionate, and I was encouraged that, despite all his medical expertise, he had such faith in my ability to heal this little baby. I felt as if a dark cloud of doubt and fear had been lifted from me and I remember smiling to myself in the delight of knowing this dear little being was the same perfect spiritual idea she had always been and always would be.

Of course, with this change of consciousness and this in-pouring of love, the healing occurred quickly. By evening Debbie was cool and lively, chortling happily as her brothers and sister kept her amused while I cooked dinner. It was as if nothing frightening had ever happened. Actually, it never had.

I find that the visible effects of some healing treatments are immediate, some are not. Sometimes we are receptive to the change of consciousness that is needed, for instance to readjust our bodies to a more harmonious state. Then a healing occurs quickly and easily. Sometimes we try to hold onto something that has become familiar to us, and a number of treatments to shift consciousness are required. Sometimes fear, doubt or self-condemnation have built up to a point where we feel we do not deserve to be well, or we develop the expectation that we should have problems in our lives. I find that even when prayer appears not to have immediate results, there is still an adjustment of consciousness occurring, and usually clients notice their lives becoming generally more harmonious. Eventually, however, the problem we treat does lose its power to alarm us, and then, as Mary Baker Eddy puts it, it "vanishes into its native nothingness like dew before the morning sunshine."

Many years ago I read about a healing of a baby who was born with one leg shorter than the other. The mother prayed diligently each day for the baby and each time she gave a treatment she felt so sure that she had seen the complete unreality of the picture of deformity as any part of the baby's true spiritual identity. With eager anticipation of seeing the healing results, after each treatment she would look at the baby but there was never any change. This went on for more than a year until one day, in desperation, she called a teacher of Christian Science and asked her what she was doing wrong. This wise old woman laughed gently and simply said, "Quit peeking, dear."

The mother realized that every time she had given a treatment, she had then looked to matter to see if there was any change rather than trusting the perfect unfoldment of good. She had been looking to matter for confirmation of the forever spiritual perfection of her baby. Her baby was, in truth, God's child and must inevitably express the harmony and balance that was part of her true identity. She was already complete and whole. Nothing else was possible.

The mother determined to keep affirming these truths and to "quit peeking." The picture of discord no longer bothered her and the image simply began to fade from her thought. Effectively she forgot about the problem until one day, when the child was two years old, the mother noticed her running fast along a beach. She was not limping at all. Her legs were perfect. The mother had no recollection of when the healing had occurred. Her expectation of unfolding good had been sufficient to ensure the child manifested this unfolding good, in perfect balance.

A question that commonly arises about healing is, "how can the thought of the healer affect the consciousness of the client?" When we understand there is no separation in the universal energy of Love, then we can see that all spiritual consciousness is one. The thought of the healer and the thought of the healed, when in harmony with spiritual reality, must both express this concord. As the healer feels the full power of love in action, the universal energy of Love pouring through them, this love energy reaches out to bless whoever or whatever their thought rests on. The healer doesn't create the healing energy. By acknowledging the presence of this universal energy that heals and obliterates the illusion of discord, the healer brings it into conscious awareness. Every time any one of us, whether or not we consider ourselves to be healers, acknowledges even just a little the power of love we help to dissipate the mists of discord in ourselves and in world consciousness.

Whether we call the idea of God the universal energy of Love or God consciousness, the message is the same. God is Love—God is All—All is Love. In truth, nothing else but love and harmony exist. We are already, always, a part of this allness, this oneness with divine Love, and we therefore inevitably express love and harmony. Recognizing this truth is the healing. The body is healed, conformed to Love's true awareness.

Nothing but love

God is Love—God is All—All is Love. Yes, in truth nothing else but love and harmony exist. I am already, always, a part of this allness, this oneness with Love and therefore I inevitably and effortlessly express this love.

Expressing this consciousness of love—seeing and knowing nothing but love—means that I inevitably express loving kindness towards myself and everyone around me. I inevitably see everything around me as lovely and harmonious. I see beauty, inspiration and joy in the symbols of love and harmony—in the landscape, in the tiniest flower, the greatest mountains, in raging storms and in brilliant sunsets. This is the truth of who I am now and always.

When I am not fully living this love it is because I have become lost in the dream of another so-called "reality," one that accepts limitation, discord, fear—lack of love and harmony—as possible, in fact, as inevitable. My task then is to awaken myself from this dream of limitation and come back to my original knowing of joy and freedom. Only by committing to living love more and more, thus evolving my ever increasing consciousness of love, can I awaken to the truth of my oneness in Love. This is the only way I can once again come home to who I am, once again find my real relationship to God, Love, and remember there is nothing but Love.

CHAPTER 18

THE POWER OF GRATITUDE

A glorious life is ... the continual experience of gratitude
Gary Zukav

GRATITUDE IS A POWERFUL HEALING TOOL. WHEN WE LIVE FROM a loving place of gratitude for the good that has come into our lives, we are open and expectant of receiving more. Feeling gratitude is all about attitude. When we trust that the provider of all good, the one eternal, divine power of Love, or God, is giving to us whatever will promote our highest good, we can also trust that this good will appear as the healing of whatever would appear to be in opposition to this good. Choosing to see our lives as the manifestation of good fills consciousness with love. Choosing to see our lives as full of lack and discord fills consciousness with dissatisfaction and all the feelings we don't want manifested in our lives. It's all a matter of perspective – the well-worn analogy of a glass half empty or half full. What we get from life depends on the perception of the viewer.

Of course some people might say this is really "head in the sand" thinking. What about all the genuine misery in their lives and in the lives of others? What about all the violence and poverty in the world? Getting locked into the prevailing thought that says we're on a slippery slide to ultimate destruction is fairly easy.

I had dinner recently with a sweet, gentle couple who had been actively involved in the protest movement back in the 1960s. Disillusioned by what felt like a futile effort to bring about any significant change in world conditions, they had come to believe it was only a matter of time until humanity finally destroyed itself and the planet. Seeing no further point in trying to create change in the world or having careers or children, for almost forty years they'd been waiting for the end of the world to come.

I shared my vastly different viewpoint that change always starts in individual consciousness, never "out there." Because we create our own reality, when our consciousness is filled with beauty, goodness, and gratitude, our thinking is reflected in a world of corresponding beauty and goodness. As we see such harmony around us we help to heal our world. We begin to see what we expect to see. Thankfully, more and more people are realizing that the change in the world we want will come from changing consciousness, from writing scripts that mirror the power of God's law of love. In short, radical world change comes from living love.

What are we expecting? Do we have an attitude of gratitude? Do we have an expectancy of good? Are our lives filling up? Or is our glass half empty? Are our lives full of problems and likely to stay that way or even get worse? What are we expecting?

How often we hear the comment, "It's too good to be true" when something wonderful happens. What does that say about the attitude of the speaker? That such wonder can't really be part of their life? Or that good won't last? What sorts of limits are set on the amount of good we expect to experience? How much good do we really expect? Can we imagine feeling gratitude every time something wonderful happens rather than doubt or disbelief?

I remember a conversation I had with my friend, Mary Hunt, a few years ago. Mary has such a rapidly expanding spiritual awareness that I enjoy exploring new ideas with her. When I first met her, she was intrigued by my matter-of-fact acceptance of metaphysical healing as the normal, everyday means of health care for my family and clients. She was intrigued that my family had hardly ever been sick, and when they had been, healings happened quickly, solely through prayer. One day, as we were talking, she had one of those "aha!" moments. "The difference between you and me," she suddenly exclaimed "is that you have a *belief* of health and I have a *belief* of sickness. I expect to get sick. You don't. It's not normal for you but it's normal for me. It's what I expect." This aha! moment was all it took for her to significantly change her attitude to one of expecting good, to an attitude embracing gratitude for health as a natural part of her life. Since then she has continued to increase her own ability to heal herself and others.

Actually Mary has always amazed me with her deep, innate sense of love. The first time I met her she was the guest speaker at a businesswomen's dinner. Although the topic of her talk dealt with effective sales techniques —she ran her own business consultancy— I was intrigued by a feeling of profound spirituality surrounding her. When I introduced myself to her at the end of the evening, she expressed interest in my work as a spiritual healer and asked if we might meet the next day to discuss it. She wanted to know how I healed. Over lunch I gave her a brief overview of how I worked and then asked her why she wanted to know.

"Oh," she said, "I've sometimes been able to heal but I've never known how." I asked her, "What do you see when you look at someone in need of healing?" As she thought about my question, looking far off into the distance, a warm glow seemed to envelop her as her eyes lit up, and she answered, "I don't see a body . . .. I just see their magnificence!" "So you see through the eyes of love," I responded. "That's how you heal. All you see is love, just love." "Yes!" she replied with excitement, "That's it. But surely it's not so simple." "For you it's simple," I laughed. "For most of us seeing only love, seeing a person's true spiritual identity, rather than a discordant physical body, is certainly not simple. The point is, you expect to see such perfection where most of the rest of us do not."

In recent years Mary's passion and purpose have come to the fore. Through her exquisite dancing, she helps clients access the true magnificence of their spirit selves and heal whatever is not in tune with this magnificence.

Imagine what will happen as more of us start to see each other in the glorious radiance of love. Imagine what will happen as world consciousness moves towards an awareness of love, towards a belief, an expectancy, of good as the natural and normal state of mankind.

As world thought expresses more gratitude and expects greater well-being, as world thought manifests more kindness and consideration, abundance, right employment and equality for all—everything that mankind generally thinks is lacking—a radical planetary transformation will elevate the race. The transformation has already begun!

What will happen when everyone starts to see how experiencing harmony is all about attitude? What do we *expect*? Do we have such an expectancy of good that it manifests as overflowing gratitude for all that divine Love is pouring out to us?

Imagine what even a little change of attitude—from doubtful to grateful—would do for us. Happiness is as much a habit as is unhappiness. We can get stuck in a habitual lack of gratitude and appreciation that becomes so deeply entrenched in our subconscious, that we lose sight of what we are doing.

Gratitude is a powerful alternative to this paralyzed thinking and it puts us well on the path to effective healing. Gratitude keeps our hearts open to divine Love's healing message. We truly *feel* immersed and encompassed by Love.

Just after I completed the first draft of this book, I read James Twyman's *Emissary of Light: A Vision of Peace*. I was excited to find another voice expressing many of the same ideas about which I was writing. I particularly love the following thoughts on gratitude and the passion of waking up to who we truly are:

A grateful heart is the most powerful force in the universe. You're discovering the passion of waking up. Remembering who you are is not a somber, quiet thing. It's like an electric current that shoots through every part of you. You feel it emotionally as happiness and joy, you feel it spiritually as peace and contentment, and you feel it physically as unbounded excitement and enthusiasm. Your awakening is a whole experience, not limited to any part of you. It is passionate. It's like the sun is exploding. It's whatever brings you freedom and joy. Your fear has been hiding this from you because you were afraid you would blow apart if you experienced who you really are. Your ego was afraid you would lose the ability to interact with the world. But it's not true. The ego made the world. The spirit only plays with it like a child. The ego makes everything serious and important. The spirit laughs at everything. Which vision of the world do you want, the ego's or the spirit's?

I love this vision of passion and joy, even play. Gratitude fires the power of passion within us. Living love becomes a true delight as the power of healing becomes our daily practice.

Expecting good

What is the truth about me now? I am Love's center and circumference. I am spiritual, radiant, ageless harmony. I am open to, and grateful for, the moment-by-moment unfolding of beauty and joy in my life. I choose to love what is happening now and I am expectant of the endless unfolding of good.

What will today bring? Because I am open to divine unfolding I continue to be amazed at the outpouring of good in my life. I am able to laugh and sing in gratitude and delight at the joy of good surrounding me.

I am grateful for all the wonderful people in my life, all the loving I receive, all the patient kindness. I am wonder and delight. I am totally unique. I am radiant joy and fun. I am gentle stillness and light. I am ALL. I am Love itself.

CHAPTER 19

WATCH WHAT YOU THINK ABOUT HEALTH

*One single moment
of insight dispels eons
of blind ignorance.*
June Spencer

A FEW YEARS AGO I SPENT A COUPLE OF GLORIOUS HOT SUMMER months in New Zealand and then returned to a damp, chilly winter in the United States. The television bombarded me with reminders of seasonal ailments such as restricted breathing, flu, colds and coughs. I could have easily become fearful for my personal wellbeing.

If we recognize that we are writing our own scripts and that we create our own physical conditions, it becomes obvious that if we don't want these problems we need to be very careful what we allow into our thought.

Many people are now exploring the relationship between thought and experience; yet many do not make a direct connection between thought and health. We need to be careful about what theories we accept regarding diet and exercise. Even filling up with vitamins and alternative health care products indicates a belief that the physical body is a solid entity that requires careful treatment. Of course we need to take care of our bodies. While they are, after all, part of our present reality, obsessing over our physical wellbeing can be counterproductive. We need to consider where our focus lies. If the body is objectified thought, taking care of what we feed into thought is going to be more consequential than worrying about diet, exercise, or weather.

Mary Baker Eddy writes in *Science and Health*, "Fear is the fountain of sickness . . . if you decide that climate or atmosphere is unhealthy it will be so to you. Your decisions master you whichever direction they take."

Many health professionals are becoming more aware of the direct relationship between body and thought. Yet I remember some years ago taking my twelve year old son for a medical check-up prior to his enrollment in a diving course. During the examination the doctor expressed concern about a throat condition my son had. The doctor was surprised that he was not in considerable discomfort and predicted he would be shortly. As we left the medical clinic my son said to me, "But I don't want to get sick." "You don't have to," I replied. "It's your choice whether you accept what the doctor said."

My response was not just based on the power of positive thinking but on a strong spiritual belief in the power of prayer to harmonize any discordant condition and to prevent the disruption of good from occurring in the first place. This prayer is not a petition that seeks healing "if God is willing." It is an alignment of thought with the ever-present power of infinite harmony or divine Love. In other words, prayer ensures that thought is kept free from the fearful and limiting concepts that cause ailments. The prophet Job in the Bible saw the connection between thought and experience when he said, "The thing which I greatly feared is come upon me."

What did my son choose to think about his health? He did not get sick. I presume he chose to accept that, as a spiritual expression of God, he had control over his health and well being.

Imagine realizing that there is nothing destructive that can ever happen to you that can't be corrected with a change of thought—you are not subject to chance, environment, aging or heredity. Increasingly, people are choosing to think in this way. Constantly monitoring your thoughts is necessary but the results are powerful.

World thought is changing as people become convinced of the power of prayer, the power of harmonious thinking. The quality of your thought not only influences your health, but it also has the power to control your level of happiness and success. You write the script for how you want your life to be. *You choose.*

Love's abundance

I am Love's abundance, the manifestation of everything Love is. Right in this moment all good is unfolding as my angels, my guides, the Christ consciousness, leads me gently towards perfect unfolding. These angel guides are my own perfect knowing, my own truth because I am all that is. I am all harmony.

When I laugh at this thing called my human life it is because my inner wisdom knows it is just a dream. This is the truth of being now and for eternity. My natural state is to love, to be all love.

My higher consciousness, my angels, are leading me into my highest knowing and my highest loving because this is my natural state. I come inevitably and effortlessly into who I truly am.

In me there is no fear, no hurt, no loss, no lack, nothing other than utter perfection. I am able to let go and just BE. My day unfolds with effortless joy and freedom as I live and love in the moment. My heart sings and my eyes light up. I trust the journey.

CHAPTER 20

HEALING IS NOT ABOUT FIXING

Reality was never compromised by your dream.

James Twyman

O NE OF THE BIGGEST STUMBLING BLOCKS TO EFFECTIVE HEAL-
ing is the belief that we have to fix something. Oftentimes,
when we perceive that something is out of order, sick, broken, or
damaged, we think we have to pray to make it better. We mistakenly
accept a less-than-spiritual and less-than-perfect reality. The key to
metaphysical healing is to acknowledge that we are always at the point
of spiritual perfection, never capable of falling from this position. From
the outset we need to see spiritual perfection and know that we are
awakening from the dream of discord and limitation. As spiritual
beings we dwell in utter completeness and Love and in this atmosphere
there is, in fact, nothing to fix and nothing to heal.

Present spiritual perfection is often a difficult concept to grasp,
and further complicated by the limitations of language to describe
concepts that do not fit with human reasoning. Perhaps the closest
most of us get to glimpsing this state of absolute spiritual perfection
is through spiritual healing, a so-called miracle, a rebirth. Great spiritual leaders have glimpsed spiritual oneness and many of us have had
some sort of spiritual awakening or moment of conscious awareness
of such a reality. Initially, we may attempt to use reason to rationalize
our experience and find a logical explanation for something that defies conventional, materialistic laws. Yet we cannot. Because spiritual

perfection is not part of the human experience, it is impossible to effectively just employ human intellect and understanding to comprehend it. But we will know spiritual perfection, oneness in Love, when we feel it.

I used to wonder what it would be like to fall in love. I couldn't even begin to glimpse the potential, the magnificence of what such love could feel like until it happened. Since then this heightened, exhilarating sense of love has been part of my knowing, or rather, my feeling. The feeling has been a part of the truth that I live each day. I can never un-know the feeling, or un-feel it. And so it is with healing glimpses of the absolute reality of perfect God and perfect man. Once we understand our present spiritual perfection we can't un-know it. Present spiritual perfection just is.

Some argue that the absolute world of perfect God and perfect spiritual man is real and the relative world of human illusion is unreal. Although I sometimes use this terminology rather loosely, denying the reality of our experience in this world of physical form is not always helpful. After all, our perception of life in this human world is our present reality. To deny its existence is to deny our day-to-day living, to negate the feelings that undergird our present experiences, and nullify just about everything we believe in right now. This can be harmful. Such a relentless and unwavering stance is like trying to run before we can walk or fly before we relinquish our belief in the law of gravity.

As we gain clearer views of absolute truth, we will naturally and effortlessly rise above the dream of life in matter. In the meantime, we live according to what makes sense to us, according to our best sense of our truth, tripping and stumbling from time to time, laughing at ourselves, forgiving ourselves, and loving ourselves more throughout the process. As we love ourselves in this way, we are able to love all humanity. Eventually we'll love ourselves right out of believing we have to fix our lives, right out of this dream of limitation and dualism. We won't get to spiritual awareness by kicking ourselves for our inadequacies and so-called failures, or by kicking others for theirs.

This is where healing comes in. When we try to *fix* what is wrong we are *focusing* on what is wrong and on what we lack. Our thought is fixated on limitation and lack. If we focus on fixing an illness, healing something that is out of order, or restoring ourselves to wellness, we are trying to rid ourselves of something bad in order to get something good. But if we understand that matter is nothing more than an illusion or human concept of what is real, then we are not focusing on fixing an illusion. We see beyond the illusion, glimpsing our spiritual perfection as evidence of the divine.

Seeing beyond the illusion reminds me of a true story I heard a few years back. A spiritual healer and his wife attended a dinner function where a hypnotist provided the entertainment. As the guests were eating, the hypnotist walked unnoticed around the room, coming quietly up behind each guest and hypnotizing them to think they were unable to perform a specific task. When the entertainer attempted to hypnotize the spiritual healer, he found he was unable to do so. The healer, noticing what was happening, had taken control of his own thought by actively denying any influence other than that of the one eternal Mind, God. Meanwhile, the hypnotist successfully hypnotized the healer's wife into believing her arm was paralyzed, preventing her from picking up her fork. The woman, in great alarm, whispered to her husband that she could not move her arm. She asked her husband to pray for her.

Now, was the husband, knowing that his wife had been hypnotized, going to pray in an attempt to fix a paralyzed arm? Or was his job merely to awaken his wife to the realization that she did not have a paralyzed arm? He quickly freed her from the illusion of paralysis by awakening her from the hypnotic trance.

The point is discord is never anything more than a hypnotic illusion. Awakening from the hypnotic dream to the reality of our spiritual perfection is the healing.

The same awakening process brings healing in every situation. For example, if, in an effort to create lasting peace in the world, we start off from the misperception that both peace and conflict exist, we are actually making a reality of the very thing we are trying to get rid of—inharmony, war, conflict. I love James Twyman's thoughts on this subject in *Emissary of Light*:

Lasting peace will never come to the world that thinks it has a choice between peace and war. The only choice you ever really make is between truth and illusion. When you choose truth you discover that peace is always present, regardless of your awareness of its presence. When you choose illusion it is like closing your eyes to what is right in front of you. And this is what it means to wake up from the dream of separation. It's like opening your eyes. Reality was never compromised by your dream. It remained whole and unchanged while you made up your own world where hatred and fear seemed to have meaning.

When we fill our thinking with love, gentle kindness and compassion to such an extent that these thoughts compose our full awareness, then love, kindness and compassion are all we see and experience. The certainty of this law of harmony is assured and healing anything discordant in our lives can be expected. When the evidence of discord changes from bad to good, we call it healing. Our human perception opened to the truth of our highest selfhood. We simply adjusted our lens to focus on what was really there all the time, and we began to see as God always sees.

Sometimes someone else's clarity of thought can help break a dream of discord. I came across a thank you letter from a client recently, describing what had happened to her as a result of a call for help. When she called me she had said "please help me" and that was all. Obviously she was in great distress. I needed to immediately reverse in my thought the feeling of danger, replacing it with a calm sense of her inherent spiritual perfection as a child of God. I didn't need to know what the physical condition was. I simply needed to understand that, whatever it was, it had no power to affect her true selfhood. I knew there was no human law capable of overcoming the divine law of perfection and harmony. Therefore, as the divine law was brought to bear on the dream of discord, I knew that the discord must be obliterated. I recognized that there was no material condition through which sickness and suffering could be imposed. What did that leave? Just the dream of discord, nothing real at all, and in that moment I could *feel* the power of divine Love pouring into my consciousness and into the consciousness of my client. I was certain of her freedom and joy in that very moment.

There was nothing more for me to do. I trusted she was free. Shortly, she called to say she was well but that she was rushing out to an appointment and couldn't talk. The letter of appreciation that arrived a few days later described how she had been in the bathroom when her whole body was suddenly engulfed in pain, causing her to fall to the floor unable to move. She had been there some time before she was eventually able to crawl slowly to the phone in the hallway and pull the phone to the floor. She managed to dial my number before she passed out.

When she awoke shortly after her call she said it was as if nothing at all had happened. Had she dreamed it? No, she was lying on the floor with the handset in her grasp. She got up and carried on her day as if nothing had happened—except she was singing out loud with joy. In truth, nothing had happened.

Healing in this way does not involve one mind fixing another, the use of mind over matter techniques, or the influence of positive thinking. Healing is not about shifting matter or the human condition from something bad to something good. It is about lifting thought out of the picture of human life as merely physical, and glimpsing the absolute truth of our present spiritual perfection. The sooner we change our focus from fixing matter to perceiving this absolute truth, the quicker we will find our lives naturally and effortlessly patterning the divine.

We have a choice. Will we view life as limited and problematic or will we picture it as harmonious and free? Once we see the range of options we're surely going to choose what brings the greatest joy and freedom, even if we only glimpse its possibilities. This is living love and understanding the power of Love to heal.

The truth in this moment

What is the truth about me in this moment? I am the complete and perfect evidence of Spirit. I am not a matter body with a limited mind inside living in a physical world. At this moment and always, I am at the point of perfection and completely one with spiritual reality. The human scene is simply the projection of my thought and I can do with this whatever I choose.

I do not need to get sucked into a belief that I am powerless to control my life. Every moment I am projecting my own thoughts and therefore I can choose this day to project thoughts of freedom, joy, harmony and perfect health.

I can't even begin to imagine all that Love has in store for me when I decide to live in my love consciousness. This is my choice and I choose it now for myself. I commit to awakening this love consciousness within me. It is in reality the only consciousness I have ever had or ever will have.

There is nothing discordant that I need to fix because the law of Love annihilates anything unlike good. It obliterates all fear, tension, doubt, anxiety, sickness, physical and mental deterioration, anything in fact that does not belong in my consciousness of love. The Christ Truth floods my consciousness and I find the most spectacular good unfolding in all areas of my life, including relationships, career, physical and mental well-being.

PART FIVE

LIVING LOVE

BRINGS TRUE FREEDOM

CHAPTER 21

WHAT ARE WE SEARCHING FOR?

As I look in all the faces I've just got to stop and wonder,
What are we searching for?....
Will you find the truth, that light inside the darkness...
Will it ever come to be that you'll find the key that will set you free....
Lionel Ritchie: Time

URING ONE OF MY BUSINESS SEMINARS A FEW YEARS AGO, David, the chief executive of a major international corporation, suddenly looked at me and said, "True, what am I missing?" At the time, the group of about twelve senior executives was absorbed in an animated discussion about what the key life values were, those most critical to leading both an effective organization and a fulfilling life. As I encouraged further expansion of the question, David continued, "I mean, I have everything anyone could ever want. A wonderful wife and family, good health, a successful career, all the money I could ever need, a boat, three cars, two houses. What more could I want? And yet there is something missing. Something important. There is an emptiness and it really bothers me."

The seminar was taking place in the boardroom of the corporation's high-rise headquarters. As I gazed out the floor-to-ceiling windows across the city and harbor, contemplating his question, a thought came to me. It is impossible to talk about life values without also talking about spirituality. They are one and the same. What this man was missing, I realized, was a foundational spiritual dimension in his life. This spiritual dimension didn't need to be a denominational practice, but it did need to be something of the spirit and soul that could fill his emptiness. Without the deep and lasting satisfaction and fulfillment that comes from understanding our eternal spiritual nature, this world of material success can eventually lose its appeal.

Sadly, it was not appropriate to fully answer David's question at that time. Discussion of spiritual things in a high-powered corporate setting could have been interpreted as flaky. However, times are changing and a response to David's question today would include a spiritual answer. In today's corporate world there is a growing understanding of the inseparability of all arenas of one's life.

Having worked with many people over the years who are ready to ask questions like David's, I am now aware of the signs. I feel sure that David was standing at the edge of his own spiritual journey. I trust that he has launched forth in search of his true freedom.

The incident reminded me of a statement made back in the 1980's by Zbigniew Brzezinski, then chairman of the United States Security Council, quoted in Marilyn Ferguson's *The Aquarian Conspiracy*:

> People are discovering that five percent per annum more goods is not the definition of happiness. Traditional religion does not provide a substitute—the spiritual quest begins for most people as a search for meaning. At first this may be only a restless desire for something more. Ultimately every human being, once he reaches the stage of self-consciousness, wants to feel that there is some inner and deeper meaning to his existence than just being and consuming, and once he begins to feel that way, he wants his social organizations to correspond to that feeling. This is happening on a world scale.

Certainly the incident with David in the boardroom was not unusual. As I discovered in my consulting practice and in graduate research, there is a rapidly growing number of people searching for the meaning of what true freedom and fulfillment really are. They are searching for answers to Lionel Richie's question at the beginning of this chapter—they are searching for the key that will set them free. I call it the art of re-designing lives—finding new ways to fill the emptiness of this inner space that yearns for spiritual knowing.

In an interview with Bill Moyers, Joseph Campbell once said,

> People say that what we're seeking is a meaning for life. I don't think that's what we're really seeking. I think that what we're seeking is an experience of being alive, so that our life experiences on the purely physical plane will have resonances within our own innermost being and reality, so that we actually feel the rapture of being alive.

The "experience of being alive." I like that.

And yet, despite the many people who are coming to realize that fortune and fame are not the key to ultimate freedom and happiness, there are plenty more who still follow the old path. They come to me sure they know what they're missing. If only they had "everything anyone could ever want. A wonderful life partner and family, good health, a successful career, all the money they could ever need, a boat, three cars, two houses…," all their problems would be solved. Could I please pray for these things? My answer is "no." I will not pray for the acquisition of things. But I will pray for a greater awareness of spiritual abundance and for an awakening of the client's understanding that, as a perfect child of God, they already have unlimited wisdom, joy, peace of mind, kindness and caring love. Clients begin to realize that when their thoughts are filled with these qualities—regardless of whether these thoughts produce the material symbols of success—they find this state of mind inevitably brings abundance to their daily lives. Their experience begins to mirror their thoughts and feelings.

The vital point here is that thought produces its effects. When we write our own scripts, thought focused on spiritual qualities of gratitude, love, generosity and so on, produces human experiences that are equally abundant, joy-filled and fulfilling. A consciousness filled with thoughts of lack, produces human experiences that mirror this scarcity thinking.

Having a sense of abundance might seem more difficult if we're not chief executive officers with generous salaries. Actually, this is not necessarily so. Oftentimes we seem to need adversity to propel us to relinquish our addictions to the trappings of fortune and fame. There's a great book on the market called *Synchronicity: the art of leadership*, in which its author, Joseph Jaworski, an eminent lawyer, describes his spiritual journey to such awareness. Like my client, David, Jaworski felt that, despite having "made it" financially, there was something really missing in his life. He also noticed that other successful people of his generation were feeling the same,

> ....they were not really living. They were not truly free. They wanted to step out and make a difference, they wanted to contribute, but they were immobilized by fear and by the need to have more and more material goods. It was the need to 'have' instead of to 'be'.

People, he realized, were not so much afraid of dying as of never having really lived or made a difference in the world.

> ... I knew I had to have the freedom to be myself, my highest self, and that nothing could stand in my way if I really wanted it.... Over time I came to see that the boundaries we create in this life are imaginary; they don't exist.

The freedom to be ourselves, our highest selves, is the true freedom we're searching for. All of us create boundaries of limiting beliefs such as "I'm not good enough," "I'm not clever enough," "I'm not patient enough," "I'm not the right shape, the right height, the right color, the right age." "Some people have all the luck." "I'm a loser." "If only. . .." Each of us must understand that we construct our own reality. We each create our own boundaries and limits. While we have every right to make these choices, we do not have to claim anything but harmony unless we want to.

Right here, right now, we can change our reality. We can create a reality that includes harmony, abundance and freedom. When we do this we are living love and we inevitably find the true freedom we are searching for. We find the key that will set us free.

Seeing my own thoughts

A problem is only ever in thought. The answer to all problems is therefore entirely in my own consciousness. When I see this, my reformation, my re-forming, begins. This does not involve willpower or a need for self-correction or an attempt to get over something. It is simply a no-doubts knowing, as effortless as my knowing that the sun will rise each morning and set each night.

This no-doubts knowing is instinctive as I become conscious of my true spiritual selfhood, perfectly formed and harmonious. The ensuing sense of unrest is also instinctive as I feel the urge to escape from anything that is either not good in my life or does not align itself with my new, uplifted perspective. I no longer accept just getting by. This process of "consciousness reformation" lets go of old habits, fears, limitations, discord of every sort which have no place in the kingdom of heaven, divine Love, within me.

As I recognize the Christ consciousness as my consciousness, what appears is a transformed and re-formed body and mind, the highest human manifestation of the God-like qualities of love, joy, beauty, harmony, balance, fulfillment and perfect understanding.

I see my own concepts. I choose these concepts of love, joy, beauty, harmony, balance, fulfillment and perfect understanding. I no longer accept discord, dis-ease, disruption, frustration, confusion, guilt, fear, as anything more than a dream, a mistaken belief that good and evil exist side by side. In the infinitude of the one power of perfect Love, discord simply disappears from consciousness and can never again touch me.

I acknowledge that I manifest balance, order, lightness, energy, vitality and joy as qualities of my eternal spiritual perfection.
I accept nothing less than perfect love, joy and fulfillment in my life.

(more)

I am learning to BE rather than to DO.

I am able to help others only to the degree I help myself. Seeking love or joy or abundance is simply claiming what is already mine. When I see this, I will stop searching for something I think I lack. By wanting something, I believe I lack it. I am denying its present existence. When I stop wanting it, and claim that all abundance is mine naturally because I am the very evidence, the manifestation, of the infinite abundance of divine oneness, I have whatever will enable me to manifest this oneness, the allness of divine harmony, in my human experience.

My standpoint is perfection—perfect God and perfect man— nothing needed, nothing desired, everything already mine. Unbelievable abundance is the outcome. This is the law of Love in operation.

CHAPTER 22

HEALING LACK

MANIFESTING ABUNDANCE

What I want, what I need, I already have. It is up to me to mani-fest it. I choose what I want to see. Thought is the real. The physical is the illusion. Ironical, ha? I am creating an entire world from my imagina-tion—anything I want.

THIS QUOTE, FROM THE ROBYN WILLIAMS MOVIE, "WHAT Dreams May Come," prompted me to write the following healing treatment for myself in 1999:

Right now I have everything. If I don't know this it is because I have a consciousness of failure, inability, poverty or lack. It is impossible to manifest success, ability and abundance so long as my consciousness holds onto limitation. It is impossible to change the manifestation of these things from the outside, since consciousness will create experience, no matter what I do. The moment a thing ceases to exist in my consciousness it will no longer have form or body; it will cease to exist at all.

When I quit *thinking* failure, inability and lack, these concepts will no longer exist in my experience. In contrast, when I fill my consciousness with thoughts of harmony, success, ability and abundance, these will manifest in my experience. Thought and manifestation are simultaneous.

I see a need for caution here —"be careful what you ask for, you just might get it." The power of thought can manifest its intentions in ways that ultimately may not be for my highest good.

If I am praying simply for the highest manifestation of harmony, regardless of a particular outcome, then my prayers will be answered in whatever way best brings such harmony. If I am unwittingly asking for things that would not create harmony in my life, even if I think they would—if I am trying to define exactly *how* I want abundance to be expressed, *who* I want in my life, *where* I want to live, or *what* job I want—then I pray that my prayers be not answered! I trust that the "how, who, where, what" symbols will appear in whatever is the best expression of goodness in my life.

When I am open to the highest unfoldment of abundance in my life and trust God, infinite divine Love to supply all good, all joy, all harmony, it will appear in ways beyond even my wildest imaginations. The source of infinite harmony is infinite. What can be greater than that?

I do not believe that God is a superhuman person watching my every move and listening to my every request. Rather, God is quite literally the atmosphere of infinite harmony surrounding me and the entire universe of my consciousness. All good already exists. In fact, because God is Love, only good can exist. There can be no discord, disruption or lack in infinite harmony. Therefore, such struggles are simply my own lack of acceptance of good. It is my task to see what God has already created to allow harmony to be manifested in my consciousness, and therefore in my life.

Gratitude for abundance is the key to manifestation. Is my consciousness full of joy for what I already have or full of disappointment for what I don't have? A consciousness full of gratitude for the abundance I manifest creates more abundance. A consciousness full of disappointment and frustration over what I lack creates more lack. Furthermore, the more I settle for what is "just adequate" the more I limit what is possible. My poor vision of what belongs to me keeps me from having the abundance that is already mine as a perfect spiritual expression of infinite harmony, as a child of God.

If I have a mind full of troubles these troubles will follow me wherever I go. Without the consciousness of abundance I cannot retain the symbol of abundance. The symbol is the visible manifestation of whatever I hold in thought. For instance, the symbol of abundant thinking may manifest as a nice home, a great relationship, an exciting career. When I stop trying to obtain things and see the presence of God's infinite ideas in my life I will see these ideas naturally and effortlessly expressed in the symbols of abundance I truly need, whether these are "things," or "thoughts" such as greater peace of mind or an enlarged sense joy.

When I fully grasp this concept, instead of trying to change the outer symbols in an attempt to acquire "things," I will accept that I already possess what really matters most—all abundance, beauty, joy, freedom, peace and harmony in consciousness. In this moment these states of consciousness will manifest in my life.

I need to see that I cannot run away from problems. Because problems exist only in my consciousness, I will take them wherever I go. Therefore, until the problems cease to exist in my consciousness I will continue to reproduce them. When I change consciousness, my experience will change accordingly. Knowing this, I choose to watch my thought. I choose to live love. I choose an abundant and joyful life without limits.

Manifesting abundance

I am not attached to outcomes. I trust and let the Universe unfold my highest good. I am floating gently and sometimes rapidly down the river of life, upheld by Love and Love's guides who nourish me and feed my heart and soul with unconditional love, beauty, abundance, warmth, and overflowing joy and freedom. I float the rapids and come out smiling, stronger and more trusting with every trial. I sing and dance in childlike wonder and spontaneity. My forward movement cannot be hindered.

I love to explore and discover my own truths and I love to share my discoveries with others. But unless I continue my journey of discovery I cannot truly help others. If I lose my awareness of joy and freedom and get lost in obligation, responsibility and duty, I cannot help myself or anyone else.

Unconditional love cannot contain any element of need or possession. It has no conditions. Unconditional love is simply love without any controls attached to it. All the love I can ever have is within me now. All abundance comes from within my consciousness. As I fill my consciousness with overflowing joy and warmth, wonder and acceptance of all that is within my experience, seen and as yet unseen, more and more manifests as the inevitable outcome. I do not need to outline how it will look but it will be magnificent, abundant and whole. I will continue to be surrounded by beauty, abundance, wonder and joy.

Life is a glorious, fun-filled adventure. In this adventure I happily manifest the continuous and growing evidence of my joy and freedom from limitation—because I am not attached to outcomes.

CHAPTER 23

TRUE FREEDOM IN RELATIONSHIPS

Love does not want or fear anything.
                                        Eckhart Tolle

FALLING IN LOVE — AH, WHAT AN EXQUISITE SENSATION! WE FEEL lighter somehow, more energized. Even sleep seems less important. We may feel an upwelling joy that spills over to touch everyone and everything around us. All our senses are heightened—touch, taste, sight, hearing, smell—we see beauty we've not noticed before all around us. We feel radiant, beautiful, and fully alive! All our hopes and dreams suddenly seem within reach.

No wonder poetry, prose and song have tried, for as long as collective literature records, to capture this feeling. Perhaps the feeling of being in love is the closest we get to glimpsing the immensity, the infinitude, of God's love—the universal energy of Love that can sweep us off our feet.

So why is it for most couples that this glorious feeling of being in love simply doesn't last? Because, for most people, along with this euphoria comes the thought that now, at last, they are complete. The missing piece of their life puzzle—their other half—has been found. Herein lies the problem.

If we think another person can complete us or provide the missing piece that will make our life the way we dream it should be—if we think this dizzying feeling of perfect promise comes from another person we're likely to be disappointed.

Forming co-dependent relationships with another person, relationships in which each partner comes to expect the other to keep them happy and fulfilled, simply does not work long term. No one can provide for us a sustained feeling of love that we are unable or unwilling to provide for ourselves.

In *The Celestine Prophecy,* James Redfield warns against what he calls an addiction to another person that can happen when we fall in love. He points out that when we look to another person to give us energy we effectively cut ourselves off from the energy in the universe. Inevitably, when this other person—upon whom we have become dependent and with whom we have formed a co-dependent relationship—cannot continue giving us the euphoria and buoyancy we have come to expect and depend on, we feel cheated by them. The euphoric "in love" feeling is shattered. Each of us, Redfield says, has our talents and faults and "we can enjoy those we love for who they are, and look to a greater source to meet our needs and supply the energy and fulfillment and confidence we seek." As Redfield notes, once we find our own completeness and "stabilize our channel to Love" we can then connect romantically to another person without pulling ourselves off course.

A Course in Miracles calls this need to find in others what is wanting in ourselves, the "scarcity principle."

> We love another in order to get something ourselves. That, in fact, is what passes for love in the dream world. There is no greater mistake than that, for love is incapable of asking for anything.

Loving in order to get something for ourselves is "love *with* conditions." I will love you if you make me feel good about myself, if you tell me how wonderful, competent and beautiful I am. When you don't do something for me because you are tired, have too much else on your mind, or you feel lost in your own cares and concerns and cannot focus your whole attention on me, then I will feel deceived by you. Such conditional love is not really love at all—it is giving love in order to receive love. Our underlying motives force us to search for completeness and we mistakenly believe that someone outside of ourselves can do this for us. Only we can complete ourselves, ultimately recognizing our wholeness as spiritual beings at one with the infinite, divine, power of perfect Love. Until we love ourselves so much that we feel content to be our own best friend—until we love ourselves without conditions, we really cannot love another without conditions.

Love *without* conditions—unconditional love—is deep, timeless and immeasurable. Love without conditions can never be lost. It demands nothing, expects nothing in return, does not trap us or even try to possess another. Unconditional love is a love of the soul that just *is*.

Sharing unconditional love in our relationships has the power to transform and bring immeasurable freedom. This unconditional love is the love of divine Love, it is the love of the spirit and soul and is therefore infinite in its abundance and scope, eternal—free from the limitations of time. The joining of two fully empowered and fully conscious spiritual beings can create a passionate union of souls that brings into world consciousness a heightened awareness of the real meaning of "true love"—the love of Love, the love of God. These light beings live with the awareness that nothing and no one can give to or take from the fountain of infinite, divine love pouring out from their own hearts. While feeling "in love" in this way can include all the exhilaration and ecstasy of falling in love, it is not a precarious, temporary state of mind, based on a dream of love that can dissipate the instant one partner finds his or her idol has feet of clay and is not, after all, the ultimate source of perfect love.

A love relationship created without conditions is co-created with God, the universal energy of Love, and as such, it can maintain every bit of its initial passion and euphoria. In fact, this experience of love, even though playing itself out in our human experience, brings us even closer to our source, divine Love, showing us so much more about what love can be.

Contrary to the opinions of many, I strongly believe that when sexual love is in harmony with profound and authentic unconditional, spiritual love, our awareness of the infinite Love consciousness, God, is heightened. Sexual love need not be an addiction to sensual plea-sure; instead, it can be a sacred way of uniting in giving and receiving all the qualities of pure love such as the gentle nurturing and honor-ing of another being. The spiritual connection of sexual love enables us to glimpse an experience of oneness with another being and this in turn brings us closer to understanding oneness with all creation. Be-cause there is no separation in spiritual oneness, the feeling approxi-mated in sexual union hints at the divine.

Loving another person without the need to control, possess, criticize or belittle, is a sacred task. While attaining a sustained sense of unconditional love is beyond the reach of most of us right now, we are all able to glimpse and live the vision of this communion to some degree.

When we feel unconditional love, we feel the universal energy of Love expressed in our lives. As an integral part of this universal energy of Love we are able to see that we can never be deprived of all the energy, inspiration, joy and freedom we could ever want or need. We are always filled with and radiating light and harmony. Knowing this, we are never dependent on someone or something outside of ourselves to give us what we think we don't have. We do not need to form co-dependent relationships in order to feel complete when we understand that no other person can give us —other than tempo-rarily—what we are not able or willing to give ourselves. Each of us is walking our own path towards enlightenment— towards discovering the light of our truth—and while we can walk hand-in-hand with oth-ers some of the way, no one can do our work for us, nor can we do the work for another. But we can share with each other an abundance of love, support and gentle nurturing along the path. However, if we become dependent on others to carry us, we soon find ourselves head-ing down another's path and further from our own self-realization.

No person can give us anything like the feeling of lightness and completeness that comes as we learn to connect directly to our Source —Universal Love—from which we have never actually been separated. We connect to this source by living love in every moment, by allow-ing this universal energy of Love to pour through us. The love we radiate is the overflow of the divine love poured into us. The influx and outpouring of love are infinite in their abundance.

As we send this energy of love into the world, it heals anything not in harmony with the law of Love. We will always see what we expect to see. When we expect to see all creation in harmony this is what we will see. Heaven will once more be seen on earth.

The sheer joy and exhilaration that fills us as we become instruments of love and peace in the world—as we see love evidenced all around us— brings us home at last to Love.

We never need to underestimate the possibilities of the feeling of love. The exquisite sensation of being "in love" is certainly real in its beauty and promise. No matter how glorious the experience of this feeling, it is only a miniscule glimpse of the even more exhilarating sensation of the power of divine Love itself, the power of the universal energy of Love in motion.

Feeling "in love" does not need to diminish or die once we know that this love is the love of God coming from within each of us. Even if the individual who helps us realize this feeling is separated from us or leaves us, this feeling has become our new benchmark for understanding deeper love. Once our heightened sense of love becomes a part of our consciousness of love, our *expectation* of love, then it must continue to manifest in our lives in whatever form or with whoever most nearly expresses this heightened awareness.

When we let go of thinking someone is giving us what we cannot or will not give ourselves, we will be free to love eternally. We are able to find this exquisite feeling of love whenever we seek it because we know this love comes from within us. We are the source of all the love we can ever manifest because we manifest everything that God, divine Love, is. We are co-creators with Love because we are One.

Once we know that all the love we can ever experience comes from within our own hearts, then truly unconditional love shared with another person brings us closer to God. We live love, experiencing "true love" for what it really is. We can also experience "true love" in the absence of another person as we love ourselves without conditions. With such love in our hearts, we inevitably radiate this love to anyone who comes within our sphere of influence, and in turn, we find this love mirrored back to us in whatever ways bless us most.

I can think of many times when I've left home to run errands after filling up with this sense of love and have found myself delighted at the beauty and goodness I see in the people passing by and in my surroundings. I've found people smiling at me only to realize I have been smiling. When we radiate the power of love like this it acts as a magnet that draws others to us. With this radiant love pouring from us we possess an inner beauty that far surpasses the physical stereotype of attractiveness. We embody and express the power of soul and bring sunshine into the lives of those around us, reminding them of what is possible.

Some years ago our family visited friends who lived just off 5th Avenue in New York. After a busy day sightseeing, I was attempting to get four very tired little children into bed when one of them commented to our host, Dave, that it must be scary going out on the streets late at night. "Oh no," he said. "There are lots of lovely people and plenty of nice areas where it really is very safe and lots of fun. Shall I show you?" So there we were, late at night, the four little children playing "follow the leader" behind Dave, hopping and skipping and worming their way around tables and lamp posts, singing all the while, and just making it in time to go up the Empire State Building before closing. The joy and the sense of love the children radiated to the people they passed was so infectious that almost everyone smiled back. The sense of safety, trust and community was tangible. We do create our own expectations.

In the same way we need not trap or accumulate sunshine, we never need to trap or accumulate love. Love is not a commodity or a scarcely produced and traded resource. God's infinitely abundant love is law. When we remember love is infinite in abundance we can never fear it will run out. We simply radiate the open-hearted love we feel and the love returns to fill us even fuller. When we gift unbounded and unconditional love to our relationships and to the world around us, we experience immeasurable freedom, fulfillment and joy. This is living love in our relationships.

A message from God, divine Love

There is no need to feel sad or lonely. I am always with you. My love comes to you through many channels. The love you may feel from another person—the sense of acceptance, safety and peace—is my love coming to you. Not dependent on the presence of another person, this love is all within you, and it appears whenever you are open to receiving it.

Be open to surprises. I have not abandoned you and I never will. You can find me as the Christ consciousness. Some people find me as Jesus in their lives but I am whatever you want me to be. You can never lack love. If you keep looking for a point at which you'll be happy you will miss all the ways I am loving and keeping you safe right now. The love you seek is not out there somewhere in the future. Right now, this moment, is all there is and it overflows with deep peace, joy, and freedom when you are willing to open your heart and your eyes to see what I have already given you, what you already are: the completeness of all perfection that is you.

Remember, there is no separation in the oneness of Love. You are all that I am—you are all that Love is. Waking again to know who you really are as the very evidence of divine Love, your life must explode into spectacular joy and delight. Never doubt my love for you. It is forever.

CHAPTER 24

STOP STRUGGLING AND SOAR!

One can never consent to creep when one feels an impulse to soar.
Helen Keller

HAVE YOU EVER WONDERED HOW GLORIOUS IT WOULD BE TO fly like a bird above the treetops, swooping and soaring over the landscape? What a sense of freedom!

Do you know that even if you can't fly you can still feel the exhilaration this experience would bring? How? By glimpsing something of the true freedom that is inherently yours when you remember your true identity as the full expression of everything God is. Because God is infinite Spirit, you are spiritual. Because God is infinite Love, you are loving, lovely and loveable.

If this is true, why does our sense of freedom so often seem elusive? We experience this sense of freedom briefly before it disappears and we're struggling once more to stay aloft amidst our challenges.

Could the answer be that we're searching for our freedom in the wrong place? Do we believe that freedom comes with money and possessions when it actually comes from enlightened thinking?

Infinite, all-powerful Spirit, Love, cannot create an image of herself that is material, discordant and full of emotional problems. Spiritual ideas are simply not subject to discord, unhappiness, injustice and misunderstanding. If we want to stop struggling then this is the dream from which we need to wake in order to see what is actually true about all mankind.

Recently I watched a wildlife program on TV that showed a nest of baby birds high up on an impossibly precarious cliff face. The mother, sensing their readiness, confidently pushed each of them over the edge! What a panic attack these little ones must have experienced as they struggled, turning over and over as they fell. Yet long before they reached the jagged rocks on the canyon floor below, their wings stretched out and they soared free across the valley.

What a lesson for us. Though we might not be learning to fly— at least not without mechanical help—we can certainly trust that we will eventually soar free of earthbound limitations. Even during those really tough times we experience in life when it seems as if we, too, are tumbling headlong towards the jagged rocks below, the law of divine Love will ensure that our wings unfold enabling us to fly free. We can pray to know that we are always held aloft in the atmosphere of divine Love and we can never crash. As we pray in this way we will hear what we need to know in order to stay safe and make the right choices.

My daughter, Kerri, and I were traveling across the United States when we hit a severe lightning storm. We were in bumper-to-bumper, but still fast, rush hour traffic trying to leave a major city at dusk. I could hardly see anything at all and was trying to cross two lanes of speeding traffic in order to pull off the freeway.

To see us safely through a daunting scenario, I turned to my usual practice of consciously wrapping my car in a big safety bubble of love and protection, knowing that, because all creation is spiritual and harmonious, I am safe and so are those around me. I was thinking about this as I attempted to safely change lanes. With sheeting rain and lightning coming down, combined with the spray from the road, the task was almost impossible. However, when it looked clear I cautiously started to move over. But I couldn't. I felt as if I was bumping gently up against a soft barrier that kept pushing me back. It all happened in just an instant but suddenly I realized that another car had been moving into the center lane just as I was and the driver had not seen me converging on him. Kerri gasped, "how did you miss that car? It was coming straight for you." There was no rational explanation why I found I couldn't move to the center lane other than I consciously realized our love bubble of protection, the arms of divine Love, were surrounding and protecting us. With this awareness of harmony as the true picture in that moment, I had brought the power of divine Love into action, preventing an accident.

How often we struggle under the misapprehension that life is perilous. We buy into all the beliefs of mass consciousness that inform us life is stressful, dangerous, and a game of chance. We adopt into our consciousness the mesmeric beliefs that either we are at the mercy of circumstances over which we have no control, or that we are misunderstood and unfairly treated – that at any moment the good things in our life may be annihilated.

Are we going to accept such a lack of control? Are we going to accept that a life of struggle is the life that our Creator has bestowed on us? Or are we going to take a stand for truth? Are we going to throw out all the misinformation and claim our God-given joy, freedom and peace?

In truth, we need not accept everything that comes to us through the physical senses as law. The only true law is the law of God, bestowing on us beauty and goodness.

Whatever is not beautiful and good is not of God, is simply not true, and can be reversed in our thought and experience. We never need to react to the false claims that our harmony is threatened. We are never subject to laws of matter—only to the pure laws of harmony, of goodness, of God. We express the energy and vitality of Spirit, the harmony of Principle, the knowledge of Truth, the uniqueness and beauty of Soul, the perfection and immortality of Life, the intelligence of Mind, and the joy and delight of Love.

What happens when we know this and demand to act only on what spiritual sense tells us is true? We naturally stop struggling, knowing with certainty we can soar high in the freedom that comes with living love.

Awakening to who you really are

Today is the start of a vibrant re-awakening of life in you, in your human life as the present expression of your divine and spiritual reality—this is you accepting the gift of life, love without conditions, with all its wonder and beauty. This is you accepting the gift of life, and living it with lightness and joy.

Life is about joy—no limits and no excuses for anything less. It is about listening for gentle whispers of truth and if you won't hear those, then hearing loud shouts and songs of joy!—whatever you need to awaken you to hear who you are now. This re-awakening is not dependent on change of place, work, circumstances, people or anything else because the re-awakening is already happening within you, just a hair's breadth away from filling your life with glory and wonder.

This human life is simply the evidence of what you know. You are creating your own realities. So, with what you are learning on this quest about Love and Life and Soul and earth shattering light, expect incredible things to happen. Just sit back and watch as this human life of yours is transformed into the most perfect expression of everything your heart and soul crave, long for, and dream of. Don't limit. This is a new life of exquisite beauty and fulfillment.

CHAPTER 25

TRUST THE JOURNEY

Throw your heart over the fence and the rest will follow.
Norman Vincent Peale

ULTIMATELY THE SPIRITUAL JOURNEY IS THE JOURNEY TO LOVE. It is the journey of the mystics to true freedom. It is a journey of trust.

Journeying to discover one's own spirituality is nothing new, although certainly, at least in western society, the rapidly increasing number of seekers is new. Walter Truitt Anderson in his fascinating book *Reality Isn't What It Used To Be* discusses the distinction between "the two ways of being religious." The exoteric path, he says, is that of doctrinal religions such as institutionalized Christianity and Islam which explain all reality through written scripture and are capable of serving as a complete system of values and beliefs for society. Exoteric paths usually do not lend themselves to much flexibility of personal opinion.

The esoteric path, on the other hand, is often called the mystical path and includes traditions such as Sufism and Zen Buddhism. The esoteric path supports individuals in the search for a higher consciousness but doesn't attempt to describe what the ultimate truth actually is. In these traditions truth is something people discover for themselves. Mysticism usually doesn't even have a fixed concept of God or of the ultimate power.

Esoteric religion, then, is about the transformation of personal consciousness, the path to true awareness, and this is what many spiritual journeys have in common. While the terms "mystic," "mysticism" and "esoteric," to many people, particularly with traditional Christian backgrounds, have uncomfortable connotations of magic and the occult, not to mention "new agey" views, these are useful concepts to think about in expanding our ideas around the individual pursuit of Truth. There is no need to associate these traditions with the god-less when in fact they can be very much about deep spiritual, God-centered knowing. The term""mystic" is useful in thinking about the experience-based journey.

According to Matthew Fox in *The Reinvention of Work*, "Mystics are the poets of the soul...Mystics constitute some of the most radical thinkers we have...they think in the context of awe and wonder, out of the experiential....and not just in terms of analysis and utilitarianism."

He observes that since the Age of Enlightenment, western religious institutions have neglected mystical thinking. "To think with the mystics is a radical thing to do."

Are we thinking with the mystics? Are we mystics ourselves? That is, are we pursuing our spiritual journey through deep inner personal exploration and does our inward journey foster the wisdom and wonder of the divine?

In *The Self-Aware Universe*, physicist Amit Goswami notes that mysticism involves a search for the truth about ultimate reality. Unlike participation in organized religion, this search for truth is essentially a lone journey, often taken by those who see something that others rarely see, beyond the reach of established teachings. It is about direct experience of spirituality and is often supported by healings, or so-called miracles. Such direct experiences are unfiltered by religious teachings that tend to foster a separateness mystics insist is an illusion. Goswami notes that,

> If we meditate on the true nature of our self, we shall find, as mystics from many ages and times have found, that there is only

one consciousness behind all the diversity. This one conscious-
ness/subject/self goes by many names. Hindus refer to it as
atman; Christians call it the Holy Spirit, or in Quaker Christianity, the inner light. By whatever name it is called, all agree
that the experience of this one consciousness is of inestimable
value.....The mystics caution that all teachings and metaphysical writings must be regarded as fingers pointing to the moon
rather than as the moon itself.

The separateness enters when religions simplify the teachings of
a particular mystic (usually after their death) to make the teachings
more communicable to the masses of humankind. The function of
these religions, Goswami observes, seems to be to pass on a particular
teaching to those who have neither the time nor inclination to go in
search of their own truth. In the process, he says, God is "recast in
the ordinary person's mind into the dualistic image of a mighty King
in Heaven who rules the Earth below." While still conveying the spirit
of the mystic's message, this inevitably becomes diluted and distorted.
It is also usually seen as the "one truth," the one way to reach heaven
or God, the only authentic teaching.

To the mystic the value of realizing the transcendent nature of
reality is seeing the inevitability of living love and the necessity to love.
As Goswami questions, "How can you not love when there is one
consciousness and you know that you and the other are not really
separate?"

The problem, he argues, is that most people are not mystics. They
do not understand why an absence of love actually causes suffering.
Until they understand this for themselves, religion teaches them that
if they are to redeem themselves, they must turn to God. In other
words, religion is a stepping stone along the way to becoming a mystic and understanding the power of love.

In all major religions, Goswami continues, there are dualistic ten-
dencies—what is good and what is bad, what is right and what is
wrong—and in most religions, a deification of a particular teacher or
the dissemination of a particular teaching or belief system. These,

Goswami concludes, have to be transcended in the final reckoning.

The transcendence out of separateness and into oneness is happening around the globe as more people set out on individual, spiritual journeys. While most are freeing themselves from the confines of any one teaching or belief system in order to follow their own spiritual journey, some are able to stay within a church community. This safety zone helps them trust their own heart and find their own direct spiritual experience. Interfaith churches, for instance, openly welcome people of all faiths, wherever they are on their spiritual path. Because the intention of interfaith churches is to provide a loving and non-judgmental safe haven for spiritual seekers, many seekers are drawn there in order to participate in a spiritual community. Going it alone can be hard for many.

Individual journeying usually entails a deep and earnest commitment to finding spiritual answers and is, of course, not the same as simply quitting on religion because of religion's demands upon us. Until we find our thoughts constantly preoccupied with spiritual things, until we find a real compulsion to live in love and in harmony with others, it is unlikely we will have the time or inclination to pursue our own spiritual journey. In this case, participation in a church that supports and lives values such as honesty, integrity, kindness, compassion, tolerance and respect for diversity may be valuable. Whatever we do and however we do it, living love necessitates that we follow an ethical code that encourages us to live in unity with others.

It is possible to pursue an individual spiritual journey within church, but ultimately any institutional or individual system that limits or defines *how* and *where* one may journey can impede the journey. I meet more and more people, particularly through my healing practice, who are feeling strangled by institutional religion. Often the people who leave, or consider leaving their churches, struggle with enormous guilt. How should seekers presume to know better, or even think of wanting to find things out for themselves when they have grown up being told clearly what is the *one truth*?

The seeker's big question becomes, is there just one truth that is called by the name of a particular teaching, or is there really just one truth towards which all spiritual teachings point?

I find increasing numbers of young people—particularly young men in their twenties—pursuing spiritual journeys and following the path of the mystic. Often college graduates, they are refusing to pursue careers that do not allow for deep spiritual commitment. They seem less concerned than their elders about the guilt of relinquishing institutional religion. Because I have often pondered why this is so, I was heartened to find Matthew Fox's perspective in *The Reinvention of Work.*

> The young have a holistic worldview. I have observed this personally in many conversations with people in their twenties; they are less tainted by a dualistic view of the world than people in Western civilization have been for centuries. When it comes to religion, for example, many of the most thoughtful young adults are really post-denominational. They want spiritual experience and the ethical responsibility it implies, but they are not committed to the us versus them ideology that has accompanied so much of the history of institutional religion.

> These people are generous but with their feet on the ground; they are idealists but realists too. They know that authentic power does not and cannot lie in institutions that no longer appeal to the heart and soul of their own generation.... The good news that I experience is that the most talented and creative of our young people believe that they can be mystics and prophets in the world.

Fox's use of the term "postdenominational" is interesting. The term speaks of the spiritual journey into the heart of love and authenticity, which goes beyond all boundaries and limits. This post-denominational journey is truly universal.

Breaking free of institution and the unwarranted "should's" placed on us by our tribes, our social organizations, is extraordinarily difficult—especially if we continue to live with the masks of obligation, conformity, and social acceptance. Especially if we allow ourselves to fall into the trap of separation, believing we need to compare and judge, or react to being compared and judged. When we understand spiritual reality in some measure—that all creation is one and there is no separation—we do not get pulled into reacting to others' inner conflict. We understand that each of us holds a unique place in creation and that we have an obligation to fulfill our unique purpose regardless of whether we gain our tribe's approval or acceptance. We allow others to walk their paths just as we allow ourselves to do the same.

I suspect more and more church leaders are realizing the dilemma faced by some of their members. Many church leaders are seeing that these people are not just quitting institutional religion because they think there is an easier way. People leaving their denominations say they recognize a deep spiritual yearning in themselves that can't be met in their church organizations. What people leaving their churches exhibit is not a self centered, hedonistic romp into the fleeting pleasures of a materialistic lifestyle, but an urgent compulsion to live a life that celebrates the oneness of all life and brings people together in harmony and gentle loving kindness without judgment or condemnation.

The church can support this individual quest but only if the institution gives us the permission and freedom to discover the truth within us. When church leaders and church members let go of the need to use fear, guilt, and separation to control members and are willing to provide safe, heart-centered spaces for spiritual seekers to congregate, they will find their denomination still occupies a valuable place in this brave new world of spiritual seeking.

A few years ago when I was conducting research for my masters thesis, "The Inward Journey: spiritual seeking in the new millennium," I asked a close friend, Tom, who has been on a very similar spiritual pathway to my own, what he was actually searching for.

> I guess I feel like I need to realize in my heart more of what
> I think I know in my head about what spirituality is. I want
> to come into the space where I'm really feeling my close-

ness to God, really feeling the presence and power of Love and peace just as I go about my day. So every day becomes a revelation instead of a struggle. In the end the answer is that it is all within us, the entire cosmos of creation is within us, just as Jesus said, "the kingdom of heaven is within you." That's literally true. It's all consciousness, being present in the now. It's the only place where love exists.

I commented on how it seems as if one strand of spiritual seeking is about understanding our relationship to God. The other is about finding our sense of identity. I asked Tom if he was more focused on one or the other, or on both. His answer was thought provoking.

Understanding our relationship to God and finding our sense of identity . . . we end up in the same place. We wake up to the fact that we are God, and as we do that we have found ourselves and we have found God at the same time. So at some point we realize we're not pursuing one strand or the other. We're seeing it's all one path. The path is something in the temporal realm of time and space—there's really no path, just an ascent or awakening to what is already fully present and manifest—just that we are God now, in full expression and radiance without conditions or qualifications or limitations. We resist this so much. We create this whole world around us of limitation and separation and temporality when it's all infinite and present and we're all one even as we look at each other. There's no separation at all. There's no space, no time, no gaps, no divisions.

In this world we are creating around us, a limited idea of spirituality is manifesting itself as form and we're all contributing to the consciousness that seems to maintain that. If we could individually and collectively change our consciousness of what's really there and awaken to what the truth is, everything would be instantly changed. We'd come into the fullness of our individuality and our identity.

This idea, namely that we are God, is a natural conclusion if we take seriously the concept that there is no separation in all creation; there is just oneness. Contrasting this view is the concept that we are reflections of God which indicates, to some people, a degree of separation. This "reflection" concept is problematic only if we maintain the view of a Creator God as distinctly separate from his creation, and of course this has been the foundation of Christianity and many of the other religious traditions for millennia.

Many believe that when we say "we are God," however, we run the risk of turning each of God's creations into little individual gods, each with his/her own separate ego consciousness. This, too, perpetuates the notion of a separation between God and mankind. It gives rise to a polytheistic view of creation. No. When we talk about God as the power of infinite divine Love, the very atmosphere of harmony in which no separation exists and of which each of us is part, then oneness in Love is where we find the fullness of our true individuality and identity. In this oneness, we find the deeper essence of Tom's comment that "we are God." We are literally with God, at one with God. We are *of* God, seeing as God sees.

Oneness does not mean sameness. We are not simply one amorphous whole. In oneness there is plenty of room for unique expression of harmony and creativity. As I mentioned earlier, I can imagine a bouquet of flowers containing numerous expressions of exquisite beauty. I love roses and gardenias for their form, color and scent. It would be impossible for me to say which I love most. The five physical senses certainly identify them as flowers but each is unique, the inimitable expression of the idea of a flower; yet each is part of the oneness of a harmonious creation.

Likewise, as human beings, and even as spiritual beings, we each express incredible diversity and uniqueness. And yet we are a part of the oneness of spiritual creation and infinite harmony.

Spiritual seeking, the path of the mystic that surfaces with such powerful and often controversial awareness, can put us at odds with the established church and cause much soul searching. In the end, though, we have no choice but to follow our hearts on this journey to Love. It is the journey of the mystics to true freedom. It is a journey of trust.

Goswami concludes his book with this wonderful assurance:

> "Someday," said the Jesuit philosopher Teilhard de Chardin, "after we have mastered the winds, the waves, the tides, and gravity, we shall harness . . the energies of love. Then for the second time in the history of the world man will have discovered fire." We have mastered the winds, the waves, the tides, and gravity (well, almost). Can we begin harnessing the energies of love? . . . Can we let our lives become expressions of the eternal surprise of the infinite Being? We can.

Yes! As we harvest the energies of love along the way of our spiritual journey, we set ourselves free to fulfill our purpose and identity. As we claim our freedom we will set ourselves and the world on fire. But first we must trust this journey towards understanding the inevitability of living love. How we do it—within or without the confines of a particular teaching—is up to us.

Affirming a perfect life now

Your life is perfect. Right now.

Perfection is not something coming. Look around. In the present moment there is utter stillness, presence of the Christ, peace. There is not a single thing wanting. Truth resides only here, only now, in this moment. There is nowhere to go but to be here, present with God and Love's entire universe. You are the kingdom within. You embody, reflect, and express radiantly all divinity—all light, joy, creativity, playfulness, companionship, tenderness, wonder, beauty and grace, in eternity. Your supply of good is boundless, never ending. You are the I AM evidenced. Hold to that, unwavering, and Love's universe will be revealed—seen, felt, realized—as YOU. NOW.

My friend, Tom, sent the above beautiful affirmation to me.

CONCLUSION

Two roads diverged in a wood and I—
I took the one less traveled by,
And that has made all the difference
Robert Frost

MANY TIMES OVER THE LAST FEW YEARS I'VE ASKED MYSELF, IN no particular order, the following questions:

Am I fully living life?
Am I fully loving life?
Am I fully living love?

From as far back in my life as I can remember I have had an innate and unshakeable conviction that life is supposed to be a vibrant, exciting, though often unpredictable, adventure. Most of my life this has been a largely unconscious conviction, not something I could have articulated or defended in any way. Just a deep down heart and soul feeling. This knowing didn't mean my life was always happy. It certainly wasn't, but even at the worst times, those times when I was not living the truth of who I really am and was not doing what I came here to do, somehow I still knew I would eventually find my bearings again. I knew without a doubt that authentic Love-born joy, freedom and peace are an inherent part of my existence. This knowing has been a beacon, an indicator that I was "on track" in fulfilling my purpose and vision.

In recent years, while on my spiritual journey to understand my true identity and purpose, I have come to clearly realize why I have always had this unshakeable assurance. I have always known that the power of divine Love is the only force or energy that really exists. My true being, therefore, is naturally in harmony, in consonance, with this love. When I have clearly seen this absolute truth of identity, I have been able to effectively heal whatever doesn't equate with this state of harmony.

I have also discovered in recent years, however, that paying attention to the so-called "negative emotions" is vital. These emotions—grief, fear, doubt and so on—act as pointers to show where in our lives we want to express more love—where we need to bring consciousness more in line with the divine.

Not long ago I had a fascinating conversation with a spiritual intuitive, Geoff Brandenburg, who lives in the Sierra Mountains in Northern California. He described grief as love that has not yet been given. Grief surfaces to show us untapped love inside us that we must communicate if we're going to break out of the cycle of this grief. When we register grief, we're discovering the possibility and promise of our lives while seeing that we haven't yet realized what we know could be. It's as if we know something about what is possible that hasn't happened. We actually know something about the apparent deprivation in which we find ourselves, and we're realizing we can change this deprivation. Otherwise we wouldn't be grieving.

I find this viewpoint fascinating because he is essentially saying that grief points us to our own potential to express the love that heals our perception of lack or limitation. Seen in this light, grief is not something to deny and bury within our psyche where it cannot cause discomfort. We need to pay attention to grief.

My friend, Mary Hunt, once said to me, "broken hearts are about being in love with the dream of love. Love how it should be in fairy tales is often the unreal expectation. Real love is about thinking for yourself, and finding out what thrills you, and doing something about it. If occasionally someone breezes by, sees your magnificence, and shows it to you, well that is a bonus."

The grief of a broken heart signals that we have placed our expectation of receiving love in the hands of another person. We are grieving for a dream of love that is out of reach. And yet *all* the real love we could ever want or need comes from within our own consciousness. It comes from thinking for ourselves and finding what thrills us—finding who we are and what we came here to do—and then living this vision. If, as Mary says, along the way of this journey to truth, we intersect with others who see the magnificence of who we are and mirror it back to us, the relationships we form with these people have the potential to surpass anything we ever imagined. As Geoff Brandenburg puts it, grief helps us discover the possibility and promise of how love can be in our lives. Grief helps us see the target we're aiming for. When we discover love is always within our own heart, grief over what we think we lack turns to the joy of knowing we have everything we could ever need. With this sense of our own completeness firm in consciousness, the chances are that someone who sees our magnificence will breeze by, co-creating with us spectacular new levels of love awareness. Whether this happens or not, though, our true or higher self—our link to the divine—knows that everything is unfolding exactly as it should and in perfect timing. Grief is healed and love is fulfilled.

Effective healing requires the essential understanding that, in truth, we are spiritual beings and that this human experience is a dream over which we have complete mastery. While we are so absorbed in this dream, however, it is likely that most of us will only catch brief glimpses of this truth. To stop sleeping or eating is not sensible until we naturally move beyond believing rest and food are necessary to our wellbeing. Likewise, to deny emotions as things we shouldn't have is to slow down our awakening process. For now, all emotions, the warm fuzzy emotions as well as the frustrating, challenging emotions, lead us to an ever increasing awareness of love in our lives—to the realization that love is all there is.

It is also important to understand that while we are all becoming more aware of God and man's absolute perfection, there are many levels or dimensions of existence between this ultimate reality and the earthly dimension that is our current awareness of reality.

An abundance of evidence suggests we pass through many lifetimes before fully and finally awakening to our absolute spiritual perfection—the undying truth of who we are—and no longer need to "progress." This process does not necessarily entail coming back onto this particular earth plane each lifetime. After all, if earth is a complex product of mass consciousness and a part of the dream that matter is solid substance, then progressing from one lifetime to another may enable us to create a different earth consciousness each time. Our world and our lives may look the same, or they may not. We gradually gain higher levels of spiritual awareness and so we see the forms of our "world" accordingly, in time increasingly lighter, brighter, more beautiful"—and maybe more ethereal. Certainly as our consciousness comes closer to the absolute understanding of spiritual perfection we can expect to manifest greater and greater degrees of harmony, peace and order.

In any one of these lifetimes we interact with people at various stages of evolving consciousness. Because each one of us creates his or her current and unique view of reality, patience and tolerance of these differences are required. Each of us is doing the very best we know how.

Beyond the dimension of physical form, there are many dimensions or stages of evolving consciousness where dependence on matter has been mastered. These dimensions include the domains of spirit guides and angels, for instance, who are seen or felt in different ways by many people. But even these states and stages are still part of evolving consciousness towards the ultimate, absolute realization that there is just oneness; that God and man are One in Love; that there is no separation in this oneness of all creation.

I grew up being taught that angels are "God's thoughts passing to man" (Mary Baker Eddy). Because our family would talk about hearing angel thoughts, I maintained a rather skeptical view of angels as "winged beings." And yet Eddy also says, "Their forms we know not." I took this to mean that different people experience angels according to their different religious learning or spiritual beliefs. Some people clearly see white figures with wings, others experience angels as wispy forms on the periphery of their vision. Some *feel* the presence of benign, guiding energy, while others like myself, listen for angel thoughts or messages.

Only in these last few years have I begun to consciously accept my intuitive knowing, my *feeling* that, while angels may represent God's thoughts coming to human consciousness, these angels are also very real and caring guides. I talked earlier in the book about how I sometimes talk to God as a loving Father-Mother even though intellectually I know this God to be a power— the atmosphere of Love, Life and Truth, of which we are an integral and essential part. In this same way, I now talk to my angel guides who help me in times of need. I don't expect to see angels but I certainly expect to feel their loving presence.

One of the first times I consciously experienced the presence of angels, was on a 6,000 mile road trip I took. My oldest son, Craden, had lent me his little white sports car in Boston to go discover America while I sorted out what it was I wanted to do with my life. I had no particular itinerary and was simply following my intuitions. Driving between Illinois and North Carolina one day, I was listening to audio tapes by Carolyn Myss. She was explaining how we can talk to angels and expect to get clear answers. I was intrigued by this idea as I'd never thought of angels as anything more than spiritual intuitions. At the same time I was contemplating the prospect of talking to angels, I kept glancing at the large Rand McNally map I had spread on the passenger seat. I needed to make a decision very shortly as to whether I should continue on the freeway or take another route that seemed to be slightly shorter.

There were no obvious indicators as to which would be best, so as I approached the crossroad, I said out loud, "Okay, angels, now I know I can talk to you and get answers, I need you to show me clearly which way to go." I must admit I was smiling to myself as I said this, feeling that this was a bit of a game to wile away the time. Not hearing or feeling anything from my angels, I made the decision to exit onto the other road. I was more than a little startled to find that when I went to make the turn I could not move the steering wheel. I shot right past the exit. Checking the steering wheel, I found it was working normally, and it wasn't until I crested a hill a few minutes later and looked off across the valley to my right that I saw a continuous trail of cars backed up both sides of a pile-up on the road I had tried to take. If I had gone that way I would have come to a stop just out of sight of my intended exit. At that moment I felt a strong and tangible sense of the presence of angels. I laughed out loud and I felt they laughed back.

I am glad to know I have my angel guides with me on this journey. We talk often, even though I also know these angels are divine inspiration from God. Put another way, because I am one with God, these angel thoughts are my own spiritual, higher consciousness, which already knows all. This higher consciousness is always guiding my human existence, gradually awakening me, bringing me back to full remembrance of my true identity and purpose.

I am reminded of this experience often because ever since then, when people ask me what I'm planning to do next on my life journey, I respond, "I will know when I get to the crossroads." With this happy angel reminder, I immediately feel lighter and more buoyant and the tendency to buy into other people's anxiety about my apparent lack of direction dissipates. I know where I'm heading. I'm on the grand adventure of living love, discovering the truth of who I am and what I am here to do. I am letting go of fear and the need to control how my life should look. I am never alone. My angels are guiding me.

I remind myself regularly of the questions I posed at the beginning of this chapter. Here and now, am I truly living? Am I truly loving life? Am I truly living love? The questions reinforce the crucial awareness of my true identity and purpose. I do not want to just exist. I want to live!

Living and loving fully is essential to feeling that our lives count and that our very existence here in this world makes a difference. And yet for all my lifelong conviction that life is a vibrant and unpredictable adventure, there have been many times, sometimes even a few years at a time, when I mostly lost sight of this. These have been times when I felt I wasn't really living or loving fully, just existing with no sense of purpose and often no impetus to find one. I wasn't outwardly unhappy but neither was I inwardly happy. I wasn't feeling black or white—just somehow gray and sort of lifeless. Where was my usual joy in life? I didn't know. It simply wasn't there.

Looking back on these times I see that I had fallen into the trap of what Meryl Streep, in the movie, "Bridges of Madison County," calls "living a life of details." I'd forgotten my questions. I'd forgotten my passion and purpose to love, to live love.

Over time I always re-discovered this passion and purpose to live love, and always with heightened clarity and energy. At this current juncture in my life, now able to share what I am learning, I doubt I will ever become quite as lost again. I still take plunges when I forget who I am and what I'm here to do, but each time the duration in shorter.

I am convinced that right here and now we all have the option to re-design this thing called our life any way we want. *Any way*! By aligning ourselves with the divine and seeing as God sees, we can improve our health, our intelligence quotient, relationships, career prospects, anything.

Achieving an extraordinary life, a lived life, is not about using the power of positive thinking or about struggling to acquire things we do not have. Achieving an extraordinary life is ultimately not even about self-improvement or about any process of getting from A to Z.

Achieving an extraordinary life comes from living love. When we live love we understand that our true, spiritual self is *already* at the point of perfection, *already* completely harmonious, *already* one with divine Love. Achieving an extraordinary life comes from remembering we can never be separate from the one Source of all creation. When we realize the truth of who we really are, we find we are at peace, free to BE who we were meant to be. We are filled with a deep sense of joy and energy and our human life simply adjusts itself naturally to mirror this spiritual beauty and abundance.

This is living love—awakening to the divine power that heals and harmonizes everything in our lives. Healing, as we know, is simply remembering our true spiritual selfhood as the very evidence of divine Love. Healing is witnessing our present perfection. There is nothing else to be fixed because there is no separation from our harmonious, spiritual Source. The spiritual power behind this knowing is sufficient to dissolve the evidence of inharmony and replace it with whatever represents the highest evidence of goodness and perfection.

Such healing brings the whole power of divine law into realization, awakening thought from the dream that there can be anything other than perfect harmony, joy, freedom and peace. There is just oneness with all creation, with All That Is.

Living Love means we create our human lives through our thinking and choices, and we begin to see that if we want our lives to be filled with love, joy and harmony, we must think and act in these ways. The quality of our thought will be manifested in our life experiences. If, out of ignorance and fear, we choose thoughts of anger, revenge and hate, these thoughts will play out in all sorts of discordant situations. If we focus all our time on what we don't have, on what we wish we had, we simply create more evidence of that upon which our thought is fixed: lack and limitation. And if we focus on the beautiful and good, on expressing an abundance of kindness, patience, gentleness, whatever expresses love most fully, we create a life that is beautiful and enriching.

It is unnecessary to outline how this life should look, what we need to have and who we need to be with. These things take care of themselves in ways beyond even our wildest dreams.

Keep affirming your deep knowing and the inspiration that comes to you as you journey on. Write these affirmations down, paint, draw, collect treasures, do whatever it takes to remind you of your purpose. Well into my journey now, I have accumulated numerous journals and treasures to remind me of my mission when I lose my way.

As we remember what is really going on, as we understand more of how we create our own scripts, we can play with this life, we can laugh at it. When the pressures of the day start to divert our attention, we may lose sight of our inspiration. We may forget the fleeting moments when we've glimpsed the truth, and become frustrated, angry, and depressed. Once more we will become lost in the dream. This is okay. Every time we remember our spiritual purpose, something more of this dream loses its power over us and we are able to extricate ourselves more easily and quickly the next time.

Taking constant time out to gaze at a sunset, the ocean, a potted plant—to just be with whatever gives us inspiration and joy—inspires us to come back to our deep inner knowing and reminds us that we can produce the scripts we want for our lives, that we are naturally and effortlessly returning to our center of perfect knowing and perfect *being*, from which, in the final analysis, we actually never left.

While my life sometimes still feels a little like a pendulum swinging wildly from side to side, increasingly I am finding balance, a place of stillness. It doesn't really matter when this stillness and balance is reached, though. All the time I am moving closer, returning to my perfect spiritual selfhood, and feeling the awesome joy and freedom of living and loving in the moment.

Despite the times of tears, confusion and doubt, most spiritual seekers, including myself, wouldn't trade this adventure for anything. Sometimes the ride is peaceful and introspective, sometimes it is wild and exhilarating. However it comes, most of the time we possess a deep, abiding sense of fulfillment. If you are just starting your journey to truth, I trust you will find courage in knowing that others are also searching for a way through the rugged and unmarked territory that besets their spiritual path.

I trust every one of you reading this book will continue to uncover your magnificent, incredible and unique identity, as well as the thrill of your passionate purpose. I trust you will continue to heal whatever no longer serves you, and that you will find you are able to help others do the same. We are all here to support each other in the joys of achievement and in the trials of struggle. As Margaret Wheatley says, "We are all pioneers and discoverers of a new world, and we all need one another." Yes!!

Perhaps you too will ask these questions from time to time:

> *Am I fully living life?*
> *Am I fully loving life?*
> *Am I fully living love?*

If you can occasionally answer "yes," I know you too will continue to find your true joy, freedom and peace.

BIBLIOGRAPHY

A Course in Miracles. Mill Valley: Foundation for Inner Peace, 1996

Albion, Mark. *Making a Life, Making a Living*. New York: Warner Books, 2000.

Anderson, S. and Ray, P. *The Cultural Creatives: How 50 Million People are Changing the World*. New York: Harmony, 2000.

Anderson, W.T. *Reality Isn't What It Used To Be*. San Francisco: Harper Collins, 1990.

Bach, Richard. *The Bridge Across Forever*. New York: William Morrow, 1984

Bateson, M.C. *Composing a Life*. New York: Penguin, 1990.

Brailsford, Barry. *Song of the Circle*. Hamilton: Stoneprint Press, 1996.

Campbell, J. and Moyers, B. *The Power of Myth*. New York: Doubleday, 1988.

Chopra, Deepak. *How To Know God: The Soul's Journey in the Mystery of Mysteries*. New York: Harmony Books, 2000.

Eddy, Mary Baker. *Science and Health with Key to the Scriptures*. Boston: Publisher, The Writings of Mary Baker Eddy, 1994.

Eddy, Mary Baker. *Unity of Good*. Boston: Publisher, The Writings of Mary Baker Eddy, (original 1887).

Ferguson, Marilyn. *The Aquarian Conspiracy: Personal and Social Transformation in the 1980's*. Los Angeles: J.P. Tarcher, 1987.

Fox, M. *The Reinvention of Work*. San Francisco: Harpers, 1994.

Goswami, A. *The Self-Aware Universe*. New York: G.P. Putnam, 1993.

Grabhorn, L. *Excuse me, your life is waiting*. Olympia, Washington: Beyond Books, 1999

Haight G.S. ed. *The Best of Ralph Waldo Emerson*. New York: D. Van Nostrand Co, copyright 1941.

Jaworski, J. *Synchronicity: the inner path of leadership*. San Francisco: Berrett-Koehler Publishers, 1996.

Myss, Caroline. *Anatomy of the Spirit: The Seven Stages of Power and Healing*. Audio Tapes. Boulder: Sounds True, 1996.

Redfield, James. *The Celestine Prophecy*. New York: Warner Books, 1997.

Ruiz, D. M. *The Four Agreements*. San Rafael, California: Amber-Allen Publishing, 1997.

Twyman, James. *Emissary of Light: A Vision of Peace*. New York: Warner Books, 1998.

Yaconelli, Michael. *messy spirituality*. Zondervan, 2002.

Wheatley, P. *Leadership and the New Science*. San Francisco: Berrett-Koehler Publishers Inc, 1999.

Williamson, Marianne. *A Return To Love: Reflections on the Principles of a Course in Miracles*. New York: Harper Collins, 1992.

Zukav, Gary and Francis, Linda. *The Heart of the Soul: Emotional Awareness*. New York: Fireside, 2002.

To contact

True Henderson

or for more information on her

workshops, talks, metaphysical healing and
life guidance,

go to

www.trueawareness.com